Pastor Search Committee Primer

Pastor Search Committee Primer

GERALD M. WILLIAMSON

BROADMAN PRESS
Nashville, Tennessee

4235-16

ISBN: 0-8054-3516-6

Dewey Decimal Classification: 254

Subject Heading: PASTOR SEARCH COMMITTEE

Library of Congress Catalog Card Number: 81-68924

Printed in the United States of America

FLOWCHART OF USE OF RESOURCE KIT

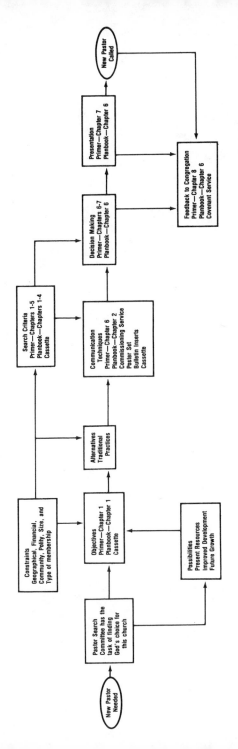

COMMITTEE OFFICERS

Chairperson _____

Vice-Chairperson _____

Secretary _____

65091

Contents

Introduction

So you have just been elected to the committee to search for a new pastor! You probably have several emotions—exhilaration, fear, anxiety, excitement, and uncertainty, among many others. If you are feeling any of these emotions, you are quite normal. Everyone who faces this task, either for the first time or for the tenth time, will have many questions.

This book and the accompanying kit are the results of attempts to help you answer some of the questions you may have now or will encounter as you move along through your committee work. Let's examine some of the initial questions that may run through your mind.

What Shall We Call Our Committee?

Several names are used to describe the committee which has been elected to search for a pastor. Among the more common names are "Pulpit Committee," "Pastor Selection Committee," and "Pastor Search Committee." Probably the most traditional name is "Pulpit Committee." This name apparently just evolved out of other developments of church polity such as the need to have someone "fill the pulpit" on Sundays. The name is limiting in concept.

In the desire to avoid the term "Pulpit Committee," some have begun to use the term "Pastor Selection Committee." While it is preferable to the former term, it has a distinct disadvantage. It can easily give a committee the feeling of more authority than most churches want to give. That is, the committee should *not* be making the choice (selecting) of the pastor.

"Pastor Search Committee" is a meaningful title which speaks to the purpose and plan of the committee. The church has charged it with assisting the congregation in the calling of a pastor. The congregation expects to have a person to serve in the broadest and fullest meaning of the term "pastor" and not someone just to fill the pulpit and the appointed meetings of the church. The committee will search for a possible pastor, but the congregation will (s)elect the person as pastor.

Throughout the remainder of the book and kit, the term "Pastor Search Committee" will be used. Discuss with your fellow committee members the desirability of using such a name.

How Did the Pastor Search Committee Evolve Historically?

It is not unusual for a newly elected committee member to feel a tremendous responsibility, to feel as if he's the first person ever trusted with such a charge. The fact is that the use of committees is probably as common a denominator as may be found in churches with a strong congregational governing polity. The use of committees to deal with needs, problems, and issues is probably the most universal factor in your church and churches like yours.

Among these churches are those with very few committees all the way to those which are operated administratively almost exclusively by committees. But there are no congregational churches which exist for very long without the one committee which we call the "Pastor Search Committee."

As numerous as these committees are, it is difficult to determine how and when the Pastor Search Committee originated. There is nothing in the New Testament to indicate that the early church used such a group. Early church history points rather strongly to the *appointed* pastor. Later history of the church indicates a gradual transition from pastoral appointments to congregational selection among evangelical groups. However, this practice has never become universal in any sense among all evangelical groups.

Today this committee is widely accepted and used by most denominations which follow congregational forms of church government. The matter of congregational government must be considered as a key point of the matter.

The historical development of congregational polity is a post-Reformation phenomenon. It has its roots in the New Testament, but its biggest growth has been in recent centuries. Until comparatively recent times, two factors were true about most congregations. First, they were relatively small; and second, they were stable in their membership.

This and other sociological factors meant that congregational decisions could indeed be made by the congregation as a whole. There was not a great need for committees and certainly not in the matter of choosing a pastor.

Historically, in groups which have been congregational, each church has its own choice of pastors. In early Baptist history, a congregation, after Bible study and prayer, would often call one out of their own midst. That is, they would tell someone that they felt he was called of the Lord to serve them. This person would often continue in his vocation and also serve as pastor.

The concept began to change in the frontier days of America when the itinerant preacher-pastor came into prominence. A congregation would call a person based (to some extent, at least) on his availability. This indicated a shift in the understanding of God's call to ministry. Whereas a church had told a person that God had called him, later the person would reveal to a church that he felt God's call.

As these denominations began to accept the idea of God's call to ministry, it followed that God would also have a specific call to minister. This being so, it became necessary for the churches to devise a method that would maintain congregational integrity, yet honor God's call. The Pastor Search Committee meets those requirements.

What Does the New Testament Have to Say About the
Pastor Search Committee?

The New Testament does not deal with the matter of Pastor Search Committees in a direct manner, for the issue was not present in those times. However, there are two related subjects which are given a lot of attention in the New Testament.

The first is harmony and doctrinal soundness among the members of the early church. Paul, Peter, and James all dealt with these thoughts rather extensively. The second subject is that of the office of the pastor. This is most widely covered in the pastoral epistles.

Since the New Testament writers placed great importance upon these subjects, it is logical to assume that they expected the churches of the future to find ways of continuing to give careful attention to them. The Pastor Search Committee is in a pivotal position to enhance church harmony and doctrinal soundness and to be an encouragement to bringing out the best in persons God has called as pastors.

Earlier, it was briefly recounted how churches moved to this dependence upon pastor search committees. With this reality of dependence, it is imperative that the methodology that the committee uses be true to biblical teachings.

What Role Will You Be Playing?

In the formation of a Pastor Search Committee, as in that of most committees, members tend to develop special roles that they play. In some cases the role is maintained throughout the tenure of the committee. For others, a different role is often used in almost every meeting.

The group maintenance roles will ordinarily be used through the total existence of the committee. This is true because these roles are built into the personality of the members. See if you can recognize yourself!

1. *The reconciler*—Works at keeping harmony in the group; helps settle differences.

2. *The inspirator*—Builds up the group by being friendly and offering praise for others.

3. *The adjuster*—Recognizes slowing of progress and changes his position in order to keep group moving.

4. *The steerer*—Opens doors for new viewpoints and keeps everyone involved.

5. *The strain easer*—Punctuates meetings with humor and avoids unnecessary tension by asking for breaks.

There are also positive and negative roles which tend to be short term. For your committee to make progress, the positive must dominate. However, it is unrealistic not to acknowledge the negative roles as often being factors.

When you are feeling negative you may find yourself in the role of:

1. *The retreater*—Refuses to participate; at least not openly though private conversations and writing habits may bother others.

2. *The subject changer*—Your attention span is severely limited, so you keep talking about topics already passed or yet to come.

3. *The controller*—This is going to be your meeting, and you plan to make sure the group goes along with you.

4. *The "other-sider"*—Even when the issue is not very important, you insist that the "other side" be aired. You play the devil even though there is nothing to advocate.

5. *The executioner*—Your way or none. You not only strongly disagree but, if pressed, will embarrass or attack the person disagreeing.

When you are objective enough to have the progress of the Pastor Search Committee at heart, you will tend to fill the role of:

1. *The prime mover*—Your thinking is sharp. Problem-solvers, always beneficial to the group, keep coming to mind.

2. *The position setter*—As the committee struggles with an issue, you are able to state clearly a position which is acceptable.

3. *The perfector*—Others' suggestions are taken and broadened or sharpened in a manner which is appealing to the group.

4. *The problem prober*—You seek to find why a problem has arisen. State it in new terms. Illustrate. Offer new alternatives.

5. *The prompter*—The group is kept moving toward a decision on the issue at hand, and the decision is reviewed for final agreement.

Of course, there is even danger in overplaying a positive role. Dominating a particular role is acceptable only when the group accords you that privilege.

What Resources Are Available to Help Me Serve in This New Role?

Until now, the newly elected committee has had few resources to help it identify its role and function and give it direction. Many committees have been elected, commended, and condemned in endless cycles without fully understanding why and how they should function.

When a church elects a Pastor Search Committee, it is taking a very significant action. Yet it is asking this committee to carry out this tremendous task with a minimum of resources. To compound this problem, often the resources available are not given to the committee or even made available.

The purpose of this book and the kit which accompanies it is to provide resources for Pastor Search Committees. This reinforces the implication that materials are needed for such committees. More is implied than just the need of materials. Implicit in the very subject of this book is the idea that a methodology can be developed and used by committees as they use the materials.

The resource kit is developed around the methodology. If a committee follows the methodology as outlined in the objectives (see chapter 1), then the materials will serve as guidelines. All materials are carefully developed to correlate with the other parts of the resource kit. This is done purposefully. As the practical needs of a Pastor Search Committee are met, foundations are established which will ensure quality work throughout the tenure of the committee.

Where Is the Place of the Holy Spirit?

It has been forcefully indicated that this is a book of methodology. Don't let that be a deterrent. The basic premise of this book and all related materials is that they will be used under the leadership of the Holy Spirit.

In fact, if a committee is not working under the direction of the Holy Spirit, there is not much good these or any other resources can do for them.

There are places in the procedures which are intended to strengthen the spiritual ties of the congregation as well as the committee. Since these are not prominent in every chapter, it could be wrongly surmised that they are absent altogether.

Committees who have used the basic plan of this book have concluded that they have experienced Christian growth. The churches also report favorable strengthening of their fellowship.

Who Will Benefit from This Plan of Action?

With the place of the Holy Spirit firmly established, it is now possible to give consideration to *who* will be seeking the Spirit's leadership and guidance as this approach is used for finding God's choice for your church.

Naturally, the Pastor Search Committee is the group who is going to get the most direct benefits from using the resources of this book and the total resource kit. A second group is pastors, including those presently in a place of service and those seeking one. The third group is the churches. Each local church has the potential to be helped as its need arises. However, churches in general should be strengthened over the long-term use of these and supplementary resources.

Pastor Search Committees generally have not known how to do their job in the most effective manner. They have been asked to do their task without training except possibly in the experience of having served before. Previous service done without training is a dubious benefit, at best. Committee members may have worked with a group who did a poor job. If, by chance, they had limited consultation available from a denominational worker, more often than not even that person had not been trained in how to help the committee in its methodology.

These same committees are asked to do their jobs with limited resources. There are some books which are helpful. Articles appear regularly in literature of various denominations, but no other aids are ordinarily available.

These limitations under which Pastor Search Committees have been asked to work make it very difficult to do a good job. Further, a committee who does a poor job will often help the church find a pastor poorly suited to their needs. Such relationships ordinarily result in short and unhappy pastorates.

It is logical to assume that most churches want a pastor best suited to their needs and capabilities. Yet it has just been concluded that this often does not happen because pastor search committees have not been the beneficiaries of adequate training and assistance. Of course, the help has to be accepted when offered.

The key is the kind of help which is available. The material in this book and resource kit has several features.

(1) *It is practical.* A Pastor Search Committee can use this material on its own and do a good job. On the other hand, when denominational help is available, it will complement that help.

(2) *The materials are understandable and usable without the members having a theological education or a degree in research.* Diligent effort is required, but this is a reasonable expectation.

(3) *A variety of resources is offered.* These resources offer a change of pace in the schedule and get at the problems from different perspectives. This speaks to the various backgrounds of committee members and the ways in which they benefit from training procedures.

The second group to benefit is pastors. Some persons called to this task have not yet had the opportunity to serve as pastors. They certainly need help in knowing how to relate to pastorless churches. Others have had experience in pastoring, but the greater part of this experience is best described as unhappy. They need to know how to relate to Pastor Search Committees in such a way as to break this cycle. Even happy pastors wish for a healthier way to relate to churches seeking pastors.

As strange as it seems at first, pastors can best be helped by helping Pastor Search Committees. Until a committee is able to do an effective job, the most able prospective pastor is limited. Conversely, if a person can study how a Pastor Search Committee should function, he will be able to relate to a committee more effectively, regardless of its level of competence.

Though the church elects the Pastor Search Committee, the committee tells the congregation how it can be of the most help. This is paradoxical but true. These materials give suggestions about communicating with the congregation and actually encourage it because it benefits all concerned.

You have some exciting days ahead as you serve on this committee and seek to find an orderly and satisfying manner of searching for God's choice for your church.

1

Finding Itself—the Committee's First Priority

"When I was elected by the church to serve on this committee, I didn't know if I was physically up to it," said Jim Franks. Now Jim is a healthy, active man at the height of his career, but he was not being facetious. He had served several years ago on a "pulpit" committee whose plan of action somewhat resembled a balloon rapidly losing its air. That committee had gone in every direction for eleven months and had never followed a definite plan of action.

Each week was a new experience without any particular connection to what had happened previously and with no premeditated action or relation to what would occur during the next week. It is no wonder that Jim had reservations about his physical ability to serve. Those committee members had needlessly abused themselves by traveling too much and had probably taken much longer to do their job than was necessary.

One very definite trait of that committee is recognizable in most Pastor Search Committees. That is, too many committees attempt to do their task without a plan of action. They are trying to reach "cruising speed" without going through first and second gear. The result is a lot of sputtering along which instills doubt, misgivings, and sometimes fear in the committee members, if not the church members.

A Design for Action

In order to avoid these pitfalls, a committee designs a game plan. In a game plan, it is as important to plan for the final stages of the game as it is the beginning moments. The effectiveness of a game plan depends a lot upon the ability of the team to function as a unit. Team members must be committed to stay with the plan unless there is a very strong reason to change.

Translated into the work of your Pastor Search Committee, this means that the group is going to take a look at its total task before starting any of it. Also, you will find ways to strengthen your own rapport and understanding of one another so you can move in unity on all matters. Further, you are going to follow the guidelines you set out for yourselves unless you become convinced change would be significantly better.

Establishing an Information Base

"Even though part of our committee has had previous experience on similar committees, we are still at a loss as to what we need to do first," confessed Mr. Bisbee. "When I became chairman, I asked the members with prior experience for ideas about how to get off to a good start. They said they just did whatever previous committees had done. They took the first reasonable-sounding recommendation and went to hear the person preach." Mr. Bisbee continued, "I believe there has to be a better way."

Deciding upon objectives for the committee is a better way to begin. A committee with objectives will always have a purpose in its meetings. You will be able to take logical steps which will keep you on your overall target of finding God's choice for your church.

Some possible objectives would be:

1. Reach general agreement as to the committee task, and then set basic ground rules to follow.

2. Structure a systematic approach for screening recommendations of prospective pastors.

3. Devise a plan of communication with the congregation which includes sharing how the committee will function and when reports are to be expected.

4. Formulate the procedures for hearing and conducting inter-

IF the church appears well organized
and goal oriented then pastors
with similar qualities will apply

views with the prospective pastor.

5. Research, organize, and outline for presentation the necessary information about the church which will be of value to possible pastors.

6. Devise an appropriate overview of the community served by the church and show how the church relates to the community.

7. Agree upon the guidelines which will be used in making the transition from a positive, responsive interview to a possible call.

8. Develop a carefully arranged presentation of the prospective pastor to the congregation.

9. Reach agreement about what is involved in the termination of the work of the committee.

These objectives will be interpreted and developed as you continue through the book. If these meet the needs of your committee, the task becomes one of personalizing them to your own situation.

A second aspect of getting off to a good start is the matter of communicating with the members of the congregation about the type of pastor desired. It is often said, "We're typical church members; that's why we were elected to this committee." A committee which takes this stance is misleading itself. People are elected to Pastor Search Committees because they are *special* in some way to the congregation. They are not typical!

This means that the committee must examine its own perceptions of the "right" pastoral type and then check the congregation for its ideas. When this is done, the results are compared to see how closely the thinking of the committee correlates to that of the general church membership.

The committee must approach this in one way and then work with the congregation in a different manner. Your purpose is to find the consensus of your committee membership concerning what the pastor's time priorities and personal qualities should be. In moving toward this consensus, individual committee members will have time to express personal views. It is important to move on through these personal ideas to consensus because this gives your committee unity for future work. It helps the committee avoid the trap of having one or two members holding out later for a certain trait in a pastor.

This is particularly true for the Pastor Search Committee in a church which has had any type of unhappiness with the previous pastor. It can also happen where a controversial matter has been present even if the pastor was not directly involved.

Max Rossman, chairman of the committee at Fellowship Church, was explaining how he took care of the issue. "I know how to neutralize Joan Lewison, so when I am forced to do so for the sake of the committee, I don't hesitate at all. This is a part of my professional training, and I think I should use it on the committee just like anywhere else." He was not being defensive; rather, he was simply explaining how he dealt with a problem which plagues many Pastor Search Committees.

People who know Joan Lewison do not dislike her. The congregation liked her well enough to elect her to serve on the committee. If they could analyze their thinking, they may have elected her because they felt they owed it to her or would upset her if she were not elected. She had been very outspoken on many issues in recent years. She was almost always in the minority but had developed something of an aura about herself with the congregation.

Max had steeled himself against this and as soon as he saw her in action in the first committee meeting, he had determined that he would use his skills to keep her from dominating the committee.

Meanwhile, over at Providence Church, Rob Strange was almost beside himself. "We have been without a pastor for nine months, and we are no closer to getting one than when we started. It is not because we have not had opportunity. Some of the finest pastors in our denomination have been interviewed and have appeared to be very interested in our church.

"However, every time we have voted about considering these persons, we have had a split vote. The truth of the matter is that we have two very strong personalities who always vote against each other. I don't believe they deeply dislike each other. At any rate, I don't know how to handle the situation."

These may appear to be different problems; but in reality, they go back to the same root cause. A committee cannot expect unity without working for it. This is true even in churches where the fellowship has been great. The Pastor Search Committee will have unity of spirit but will have to work for its unity of purpose as it relates to a pastor.

As in the case of Joan Lewison, congregations often elect persons because they believe divergent views should be represented. This is not bad if those views are not polarized to the extent that Max Rossman feels he has to neutralize a person or Rob Strange is completely frustrated.

Your key is committee consensus.

You will need to develop a plan for your committee in reaching this consensus on the traits you desire in a pastor. What kind of person are you looking for? An outstanding pulpiteer? One who visits? One who ministers to the sick and distressed? One who will be active in community affairs? You probably desire all of these traits as well as many others. However, it becomes necessary to prioritize in order to find the person you are looking for. Few people, if any, possess to a maximum degree all the traits desirable in a pastor.

A process for reaching consensus is described and outlined in the Committee Planbook. This exercise is usable by any committee in any size of church. It is adaptable as far as time required to complete the process is concerned.

When your committee has decided what characteristics it desires in a prospective pastor, it is important to find out if this is the kind of person the congregation wants. A questionnaire or other type of survey device may be used to poll the congregation on traits they may expect in their pastor.

An instrument designed for this purpose is included in the Committee Planbook. It is most effective if used on Sunday morning and can be completed in ten to fifteen minutes. The questions raised are not exactly the same as those in the committee exercise, but the results are definitely comparable.

It is important to keep in mind the purpose of a questionnaire. It is not to find what each member of the congregation individually desires, but to give each member the opportunity to have a part in expressing the congregational consensus.

Often the mistake is made of asking questions which tend to divide rather than unite. This is usually done innocently under the guise of letting the people speak so that controversy can be settled before a pastor is called.

"We need to ask the people whether they want a pastor who emphasizes a certain doctrinal position," argued Tom Basik.

"No, we ought to be more interested in age and education," responded Frank Moro. "After all, Reverend Jansen stayed here until he retired; and the membership may want a drastic change."

"Well, I'm sure the people would like someone who drives a less expensive car," said Dan Krause a little heatedly. "We're working people, and we need someone who will live as we do."

While all of these matters can be of importance for certain churches, the congregation's possible feelings of discontent should not be fanned. The very fact that your committee is already aware of the situation should suffice.

You should go to the congregation in a positive manner. You should ask them to express themselves about ministry priorities. A pastor who does please the congregation with his pastoral skills will cut across most other barriers.

Now you have a way of checking to see if you are thinking along the same lines as the church as a whole. This is an important step and will assure a happy beginning as the new pastor begins his work.

Putting the Frame Around Your Design

"I have been enjoying what we have been doing up until now, but I'm ready to get on with our task," intones Mr. Wright in his

45091

inimitable efficient manner. While committees can get bogged down in too much introspection, it is not quite time "to get on."

Now is the time to nail down a few more pegs which will prove beneficial to you as you move along with your work.

(1) The committee needs to make a firm commitment to use the tools and resources it has at hand—not just the ones mentioned in this book, but any others you find and believe can be beneficial. The temptation will be overwhelming later to "play it by ear."

(2) You will want to adopt some evaluation techniques for checking up on your process during your course of action. Consideration should be given to using the checklist in the Planbook. It can be used individually or as a group instrument. However, there must be agreement on how periodic the checkups will be; and these should be on future agendas.

(3) Take formal action! Adopt the policies and principles that meet the needs of the committee. Do so by voice vote. Agree to do the same in the future as the occasion may demand.

Once this is done, you have great confidence in saying to the people of the church, "Here is what we are going to do, and we want you to know how we will be functioning."

Increasing Productivity by Using This Alternative

Though one of the basic themes of this book is that you can do a better job without a lot of extra meetings, you may want to consider changing at least the format of one of your first meetings. This would be the first session in which you begin to formulate the "design of action" previously discussed in this chapter. You may want to consider a retreat meeting of the Pastor Search Committee.

A retreat setting offers such advantages as:

1. Getting the group away from the pressures of work and family responsibilities.

2. Relieving the limitations of time prescribed by night or even Sunday afternoon meetings.

3. Giving the committee the opportunity to work through all

of the initial stages of the task in a limited time frame rather than over a period of several weeks.

4. Giving the committee time to put together some of the materials that will be needed later. See particularly chapter 3.

Difficulties can be overcome:

1. "Hard to get away"—any schedule is going to take committee members' dedication and setting of new priorities.

2. "A lot of time in one chunk"—a retreat should be a time saver in the long run. It will either eliminate some meetings or advance the schedule.

A retreat is only a suggestion, but it does have enough value to at least warrant examination by your group. Even if this has to become a "second mile" effort, the Pastor Search Committee is going to be called upon often to do that in order to find God's choice for your church.

You will find valuable help in the Planbook and the other items in the resource kit.

Related Helps

Planbook

Chapter 1 contains forms and information that pertain to what you have just read.

Resource Kit

See the Card Assortment for determining priorities; listen to the introductory section of the Cassette; examine the Retreat Agenda; carry out the Commissioning Service.

2

Sorting the Prospects

"I just can't believe Dr. Love would care enough about our church to send a recommendation on such a fantastic person," was Mrs. Ary's breathless remark at the second meeting of the Pastor Search Committee of Trinity Church. "Oh, you mean Dr. Love at First Church, River City. He's the one who recommended Reverend Dudley to us six years ago," replied Mr. Cutter. Mrs. Ary's sigh was an unquestionable sign of loss of enthusiasm for Dr. Love's suggestion.

The Need for Caution

"Well, I haven't received a recommendation yet," said Mr. Marks, "but I don't want to get caught in a situation like the last time I served on a Pastor Search Committee." As Mr. Marks continued, he shared that a church member had mentioned a name to him in an offhanded manner. The member had never brought up the subject again until the committee was set to recommend another person as pastor. This member then demanded to know what consideration his recommendation had been given. The answer, of course, was "none," since Mr. Marks had never really understood that a recommendation had been made.

These two situations illustrate the types of recommendations that give a committee the most trouble. Both have one thing in common—a lack of substance which the committee can use to evaluate and begin to expand upon as it works. But they are also different in the difficulties they reflect.

Dr. Love is typical of the person who, because he has some vestige of prestige, feels he can arbitrarily make recommendations to pastorless churches. Though there has been no audible request for this service, their tribe seems to be increasing.

To be sure, such persons have the right to make recommendations. However, they should feel the same sense of accountability as anyone else. Recommendations made in an arbitrary, capricious manner are a mocking of the New Testament and of the local church's right to have God's choice for their church.

On the other hand, a member of a pastorless church often imagines that the fact of membership gives him the right to be careless in dealing with the Pastor Search Committee. A committee often encounters an offhanded mention of a name for a prospective pastor. The church members may not want to take time to make a proper recommendation, or they may not know how. The committee should be given more than a name and directions about how to find more information. If church members know how to get the information, they should make the effort personally.

"Mrs. Whaley stopped me in the hall after church last Sunday," shared Paul Whigham with the other committee members. "She said she had a recommendation for us. It so happened we were not far from the bulletin board, so I walked on over and showed her how to make a written recommendation. It seems she didn't really know that much about the person. A friend visiting her recently heard we were pastorless and told us her former pastor surely would make us a fine pastor. All she had was his name and the town in which he now lived. I explained our committee policy about written recommendations and assured her we would give serious consideration to hers when it was received. She said she wasn't sure she wanted to go to that much trouble since she wasn't that certain he was a good prospect."

"She added that she really understood our situation; she just hoped we would make an exception for her."

After other members related similar incidents, they all agreed that written recommendations were a basic requirement.

The most effective way to handle these and other problems is for the Pastor Search Committee to take the offensive. This must be done quickly because the pressure builds early to consider everyone's good idea for a pastor. If your committee has already begun to receive recommendations, place them all "on hold" until some decisions of methodology are made. This is not a time for haste.

Be Prepared for Some Hard Work

Setting up the mechanics to screen the prospects is not a difficult job. Rather, understanding how it will work and then having the fortitude to stick with the plan is frequently the most arduous aspect of the task.

Your committee will sense that it is going to take more time and effort than the usual process. You will begin to doubt the benefits of the presumed results in light of the demands that will be made. But don't let this sway you. There is a tendency to fail to realize that time and effort can be saved for later steps, and these steps can become the fulcrum for the total effort of the committee.

A Unified Approach That Uses Comparable Information

Step 1: Only prospects with written recommendations in committee files will be considered. This applies to recommendations from church members as well as from people outside the church.

This step seems innocuous enough, but there will be many who wish to ignore it. One way to help such people is to prepare forms for them to be used in making a recommendation. In fact, there is much to be said for a committee decision that decrees that all recommendations must be made on these forms. Some of the advantages are:

1. Time saved—elimination of extraneous information.

2. Comparable information received—a committee can compare like information. Normally every resumé has its own style and body of information.

3. The right information is sought for this stage of the process.

The notable disadvantage is that persons making unsolicited recommendations have to be asked to do them over.

The positives appear to outweigh the negatives. However, even what seems a negative can be reversed when a person does not believe in his recommendation strongly enough to repeat it. He has helped with the screening process.

Step 2: Only prospects whose references have been checked will be considered by the Pastor Search Committee.

This step obviously demands that references be given as a part of recommendations. The Planbook includes forms for your convenience.

"Do you really believe you can get any information of value from references?" inquired Mrs. Howe of the consultant who was meeting with the Pastor Search Committee. "When I served on a committee several years ago we made an attempt to use references and we felt like we wasted our time." As she kept talking, Mrs. Howe mentioned the following reasons why they had no success.

1. The committee felt that the references were chosen out of ulterior motives.

2. They got a low percentage of replies from those they contacted.

3. The information received was not valuable.

4. Instead of having a broader perspective on the person being recommended, the committee had the uneasy feeling that they were being coerced.

Many Pastor Search Committees can identify with what Mrs. Howe discussed. Some might even wonder if they had been on a committee with her. However, the very fact that the problems of using references are so identifiable should mean that solutions are available—and they are.

Problem 1: The ulterior motive
Solution: The basic idea of having a reference is to acknowledge that the person knows enough about the party in question to give information. It is also reasonable to expect that a person with

a favorable attitude will be chosen to serve in this capacity. This implies a natural rather than an ulterior motive.

This explanation still does not speak to the fact that a committee wants honest, straightforward answers to its questions about the prospect. Getting answers is possible, but it has to be the result of some good tough work on the part of the committee.

The first thing that must be done is to gain some control over what types of references will be used. Naturally, one cannot personally choose specific people; but by using a uniform recommendation form, guidelines can be established over the kinds of references.

There are basically four kinds of references for pastors. First and most obvious is another pastor. Second, a committee should request the name of an educator (a college or seminary professor). Third, a former church member (not from the present place of service) should be solicited. Fourth, a Director of Missions or another denominational worker should be listed for contact.

As the ulterior motive is dealt with, the solution begins to lap over into:

Problem 2: Low percentage of replies
Solution: The advantage that is gained in controlling kinds of references is kept by writing proper letters to the references. Two suggestions will be helpful. First, ask questions that acknowledge the relationship that the person has with the prospect—that is, benefit from the fact that a person held membership where the candidate formerly pastored. Second, impress upon the person that you are serious about a reply and that you are not just going through a routine. The personal touch and true urgency factors will increase the percentage of replies in a significant manner.

Problem 3: Poor value of information received
Solution: Though a step has been taken on this matter in solution 2, your committee must go further. It is necessary to give the person some information about your church and then give some

direction concerning the kind of information you are requesting.

A sheet or two of pertinent facts about your church and the community it serves can make a large difference in how accurately a reference can assess a prospect for a church. The better the material furnished the person, the more valuable the response for the committee.

Still, there is no guarantee that the reference will respond unless further help is offered by your committee. Part of this help is in the letter. There the suggestion is made that the response to the questions should be in narrative style. This encourages openness and additional information rather than simple yes or no answers.

As a means of getting more evaluation and as an alternative for the person who dislikes writing narrative answers, there should be included a one-sheet character reference inquiry. Examples of such inquiries are found in the Planbook.

"Did you pick up the same thing I did in the letter from Dr. Broad?" inquired Don Falcon. "He said that although he had been in three revivals with John Minton, he really had never gotten to know his wife. This sounds as if she may be aloof or terribly shy. Since the last two pastor's wives in our church were very warm and outgoing, we should check on this. It could cause her a lot of stress if we expect more than her personality allows her to be."

Later in the interview, the committee learned it was the dominance of John Minton which caused the situation. Nevertheless, they were thankful for the honesty of Dr. Broad. He had passed some information along which they would not have received without using him as a reference.

The factual sheet and the narrative will assure a committee of much evaluative material on which to chew.

Problem 4: The references are in collusion

Solution: Naturally the first three solutions are all going to help avoid this (if it ever is a real problem). There is one further action the committee should consider. Actually, it has value in and of itself, but it can be used as a hedge against being presumed upon by well-meaning people.

The action is to send a letter and a request for information to the person being recommended. The form (see the Planbook) asks the person for similar but not identical information to that requested of the person making the original recommendation. Examination of this information should resolve the issue of being used by the parties involved.

"I'm not sure we are looking at the same person when we compare what Ben Patton says about himself with what others say about him." Everyone on the committee with Sylvia Hunt agreed with her. "His reasons for leaving the various churches do not coincide with what Basil Estes said in his recommendation. I have concluded that Ben Patton is a person who never stays long anywhere and Basil Estes is a friend who never questions why; he just tries to help him find another place."

Not everyone agreed with that conclusion, but the committee did decide to privately study the information from both men and the references before giving a priority to Ben Patton.

Usually there will be a period of several weeks before a committee can move from this step to the next step. This is not wasted time for several reasons. First, there are other actions the committee can be involved in during this interim. Second, using the time to check references is going to save both hours and miles later in the process. It means that your committee can do a lot at home and in the church and still be moving toward accomplishing its task.

When there is enough information from the sources contacted to be able to evaluate at least three persons, it is time to gear up for Step 3.

Step 3: At each meeting of the committee, prospects meeting standards of Steps 1 and 2 will be given priority ranking. The committee will decide whether it will deal with more than one prospect at a time during this stage. (See alternatives on next page.)

If copies cannot be made of all material so that every committee member can be furnished with personal copies, then adequate time must be given for all to study the material individually. Since this cannot be done during the course of a meeting, it may mean a delay of a few days.

Though it may seem paradoxical since the information was gathered so it could be compared, the discussions should be about one prospect at a time. Each committee member will have the opportunity to express a personal response to the information at hand. After all have had this privilege, priority ranking is given.

When not over five persons are being evaluated, the priority rankings can be done informally. When more are being dealt with, then each of you should rank your top five by giving a 5 for number 1, 4 for number 2, 3 for number 3, and so on. The person with the most points then receives the top rankings.

"To tell you the truth, I dreaded coming to this meeting to-night," confessed Pat Truly. "After reading all this information about these people, I knew we had some top-notch prospects. That is what confused me and caused my fear. It just didn't seem possible that we could come to agreement and still feel positive. You all know my preferences and my choice as the prime prospect. Even though this person is not the one which the committee has at the top of the list, I feel good because of the way that decision was made. No one was negative about my choice; there were just more of you positive about another person. I like the priority-ranking plan. My candidate may still emerge as God's choice for our church; but if not, I'm sure we will find that person with this plan."

Those who do not receive generally favorable response from the committee during discussions should not be included in the ranking process. This will keep the process simple and save time as well.

As information continues to filter in regarding new prospective pastors, the ranking process continues. The same review of information is employed, and the question is raised as to whether the person should be ranked higher than any previously positioned. If there is a positive response, the same priority classifying takes place with a mixing of the old and new candidates.

A Look at Alternatives

There are two options which a committee considers at this point in order to move smoothly into Step 4.

You can give consideration to several persons concurrently, or you can choose to proceed with only one person at a time. At this juncture of the process, either alternative is fair. However, it is best for your committee to determine which choice suits it best and to stay with it.

When the preference is to have several persons under consideration at once, then care must be taken in how Step 4 is implemented. Some ministers assume that they are the only person under consideration when a committee makes an open contact. This will need to be clarified when the interview occurs. Naturally this issue is moot when your committee's option is to be in contact with only the highest priority prospect.

Caution: In neither case does the committee suspend the process of gathering information on additional recommendations.

Step 4: When a prospect becomes a top priority condidate, he will be personally contacted by the committee chairperson to determine his interest and availability.

This step clears the air. Though some committees may think it incredible, there are ministers who are happy and content and would rather not even give consideration to changing pastorates. There is a real temptation when this happens to use a bit of coercion, but you should resist doing that. The favorite form of spiritual coercion is taking the person to task for not being willing to pray about the matter. (How does one know when another has prayed?) Others seek to compel consideration by mentioning prestige, money, honor, and so on.

Mr. Franklin was reporting to the Pastor Search Committee about two recent contacts. "You all know that Dave Ewing was given top priority at our last meeting. You will also recall that we chose not to make direct contact with our prospects by asking them for personal data. When I called Mr. Ewing, this was the first he knew about being under consideration. He was very courteous, but he quickly declined consideration. I shared with him how impressed we were with his credentials, but he was firm in his conviction that he should not talk about leaving his present position.

"Fortunately, since we had determined that Peter Burton was our second strongest condidate, I was able to contact him. Here is what I learned . . ."

For the person who does express interest, this is the time to briefly outline the methodology the committee is using. Since this first contact is normally by telephone, the sharing is limited. If no problems arise, the way is clear for Step 5.

Step 5: If the person is interested, a date will be agreed upon for the committee to hear the candidate preach and to have an extended interview.

There is one sure remedy for the discomfort a committee feels when it visits a church to hear a prospect—go only by invitation. Of course, the whole church is not going to give you an invitation; but if the pastor does, the burden of responsibility shifts from the committee to him.

This is one of the reasons you contact a priority prospect before going to hear him. Other reasons are that there can be assurance that a special program of the church such as a stewardship campaign or a revival preparation service will not be infringed upon. Also, the committee can be fully prepared if they have two or three weeks' notice; and the prospect will have his schedule planned to give the committee maximum use of time.

There are naturally objections to the idea of advance notice. After removing the variations the objections boil down to these:

1. The prospect will use his best sermon—his "sugar stick." Answer: Your purpose is to find out how well the person *can* preach! If he is at his best (and every opportunity has been given), then it is easy to evaluate. If he is good, he can be heard again. If

he is terrible, a committee won't feel bad about acknowledging it.

2. The prospect will be ready for the committee; the committee won't experience a "natural" situation. Answer: What is a natural situation? What would be one in the Pastor Search Committee's church? In truth, by trying to force a natural situation by a surprise appearance, a contrived or artificial atmosphere often develops. Realistically, at this time the committee wants to be as informed as possible about the potential candidate. They also want the candidate to be prepared to discuss with them the possibility of a future ministry together. This comes about best when freedom and openness abound.

The positive results of this step far outweigh any negative factors. A committee that uses this step can expect the following:

1. *Anticipation*—Having thoroughly investigated the prospect to this point, and having cleared away the possibility of interfering in the church to be visited, a committee will anticipate rather than dread the situation.

2. *Expectation*—By adding the sense of being led by the Spirit to the previously mentioned factors, a committee will expect spiritual blessings regardless of what else occurs.

3. *Gratification*—Doing things right means that when the committee and the prospect part that day, they will both be able to express thanksgiving to the Lord for the experience of working together in his name.

Let It Be Said Again

Screening is hard work! A committee must accept this fact but at the same time look at the possible results of that toil.

The committee that sees the whole picture will enter into its work joyfully. It will do so because it knows that some of the later tasks will be easier and that its overall goal of searching for a pastor is heavily dependent on thoroughness at this point.

Related Helps

Planbook

See chapter 1 for sample materials as well as more specific directions for carrying out the screening process.

Resource Kit

Listen to the Cassette for reasons to be patient in this stage of your work; if you are scheduling a retreat, examine the Retreat Agenda and coordinate it with the first chapter of the Planbook.

3

Probing for Further Information

In chapter 2 the emphasis was upon the mechanics of the process with some attention also given to rationale for each screening step. In this chapter we will seek to deal with the art of relationships.

When you look back upon the work your committee has done after a pastor is called, you will be amazed to find that built into all of those processes you went through was a series of relationships with people who assisted you in numerous ways.

Later chapters will be concerned with relationships with prospects. At this point we want to focus on the people who help determine who the best prospects are. This can be done best by following the format of the screening process in chapter 2.

The Art of Getting the Kinds of Pictures You Need

Recommendations are a vital part of the pastor and church coming together. Unfortunately, the kinds of recommendations that are given are not always beneficial. Most of the time this is because the church members do not know what you need in a recommendation.

What you want them to do is paint a picture for you of the candidate they wish you to consider. Some people are natural artists when it comes to making a recommendation. They are able to show you exactly what the person's ministry characteristics and skills are in relationship to your church's needs. Most recommenders have not had that kind of training. They like to dabble in the art of making recommendations, but their pictures leave you rubbing your eyes in confusion.

This doesn't mean these people can't help you. But first you have to help them. Your committee encourages them to "paint by the numbers." You tell them what kind of information you want about prospective pastors. This is a fairly simple task if you devise a form. You will find one in the Planbook for your convenience. It is designed to get specific information about every person recommended. Though it is specific in the sense of raising the same questions about every person, it becomes personal through the information shared about each individual.

The form which is recommended also has one very powerful feature built into it. It requires the person making the recommendation to justify his reason for saying that your church should consider this particular person. Simply stated, you avoid having to waste time on mass recommendations by someone just trying to help a friend. Even though they have painted by the number, you have not had to put up with information simply run through a copy machine with no consideration of your needs.

The Need for Some Sculpturing

The sculptor creates a picture which has thickness as well as breadth and length. This is another dimension which benefits you in your search for understanding about any person you begin to feel worthy of consideration.

It should be pointed out here that not every person who is recommended is going to get serious consideration by your Pastor Search Committee. It becomes immediately evident that some simply do not have the basic qualifications for consideration for your church. This is not to question their call to the ministry or their basic qualifications, but simply an acknowledgment that the particular person and your church would not make good partners. Therefore, references are not checked on these candidates.

References become your potential sculptors. If it is true that not everyone can paint a picture, it is certainly more veritable that not everyone is a sculptor. But again you can help those trying to help you. You are not asking for a masterpiece for museum purposes —only for some chipping and whittling which will clarify your understanding of the person under consideration.

You can help them start the chipping process by giving them the opportunity to evaluate the person's character, work habits, etc. This is ordinarily best done by using a form which calls for subjective appraisal and can be done rather quickly. Besides giving you valuable information for later study, the use of this form can also be an encouragement to go a step further and whittle at the finer points you need to be interested in about the prospect: his interests and capabilities in ministry.

> Dear Reverend Bisbee:
> A fine young man, Peter Marshall, gave your name as a reference. Please write us what you know about him since our committee is giving him serious prayerful consideration.
> > Sincerely, Sam Hope—Chairman

Such a letter is not going to elicit a sculptor's response. For one thing, it implies that the committee has settled the matter unless they hear something bad. Why answer unless something is wrong? Indeed, some people used often as references would say, "Why answer even if you know something is wrong?"

Even worse is the committee chairman who calls references and says, "I'm not asking you to put this in writing because I want you to be honest with me." Is he implying that nobody will be honest in written references? By using this approach, he also may be denying the rest of the committee the exact information he receives.

If you want your potential sculptor to whittle, you have to get his confidence. He must be certain that you will keep everything confidential even if he carves out some unexpected flaws. He must also firmly believe that you are going to take seriously all of the information he shares with you regarding the strengths and weaknesses of the person involved.

Though you can readily see the danger of taking this analogy too far, you should also be able to see how valuable references can be if you give them the proper respect and encouragement.

The suggested letters and forms found in the Planbook will prove beneficial in accomplishing the procedures suggested in this chapter.

Harmony as a Part of All Relationships

One of the key goals of these materials is to offer Pastor Search Committees guidance which can build harmony. However, harmony is necessary in relations outside the group as well as within.

This has been kept in mind as suggestions have been made about relating to recommenders, references, prospects, and churches being pastored by prospects.

There is one other group of persons you need to be sensitive to in regard to maintaining harmony: persons already on your church staff. This area will be covered in the fifth chapter in some detail as well as by brief references in chapters 6 and 7.

Providing a Good Model

When you begin to correspond with persons making recommendations or with persons given as references, you will find that a reciprocal relationship enhances your efforts! That is, when you reply to an unsolicited recommendation and you are asking for more and difficult information, you will want to say, "Here is some data which will help you reply to our request."

This is your opportunity to give a lesson in painting or sculpting without being obvious. You do it by providing good models. Both recommenders and references need information about your church and your community in order to be able to respond intelligently to your inquiries. Their need becomes your advantage.

There are going to be other persons who need this kind of information also. They are the individuals who become priority prospects. (See chapter 2.) They will actually need more information than the recommenders and references. They also usually need it later, but you can save time by providing for the prospects and then condensing the materials you furnish the others.

Your church is special or you would not be a member of it. But because it is special, you may not have a true picture of it in your mind. This could cause complications by your unintentionally misleading those you are sharing with.

Perhaps the most basic question a Pastor Search Committee asks of itself is, "What is our purpose as a church?" Many churches have a confused mind when it comes to their purpose in the world and their role in the community. To clarify your mission as a people of God in a specific time and place goes a long way in helping to understand what kind of pastor you need.

1. Your committee may begin with a review of the church's history. It is good to collect such information as a brief summary of the origin and development of the church, significant factors which affected growth, and past milestones of the church. This information is helpful in understanding not only where the church has been, but also where it is and where it seems to be going.

2. Also helpful in understanding your church are some important statistics. Such statistics include church membership, number of additions by baptism and letter, average attendance at each of the services and organizational meetings, amount of church budget, and the offerings actually given. These statistics are not simply static numbers, but can become dynamic pieces of information.

3. Answers to questions such as the following will give valuable insight into the attitudes, desires, strengths, and weaknesses of your church body.

"Why has church attendance been declining the past five years?"

"Why are the number of conversions up so much this year?"

"Why is the young people's group growing so rapidly?"

"Why has the budget stayed the same for the past three years?"

4. Your Pastor Search Committee will also want to analyze the constituency of the congregation. You will determine the various age groups and their sizes, the occupations and interests of the members as well as their educational level and incomes. From the spiritual side, questions should be answered about the number of tithers, the number and quality of real committed church members, and the leadership ability of the church membership.

5. Another important question your committee will ask is, "Is our church oriented to the future?" Too often a church has some great event in their past which keeps it from looking ahead and which destroys its vision to reach the community for Christ. If your church is oriented to the past, your committee will need to search for a person who can help reorient it to the future.

6. All of these previous areas of investigation naturally lead to a self-evaluation of the programs of your church. What are the various organizations of the church? How are they supported? What are your ministries? Do they meet the needs of your church and community? How do they relate to the central purpose of your church? A church that has their programs growing out of their purpose and is striving to meet needs is on the right track and will have a good chance at successful ministry. Too often, however, a church program exists as an end in itself, the members having lost sight of the church's mission.

The church evaluation by your Pastor Search Committee not only reveals the strengths and weaknesses of the church, but it helps answer your committee's most important question: "What kind of pastor do we need?" Such an investigation is not only helpful; to the committee who is genuinely concerned with finding the right person, it is imperative!

Similarly, it is wise to make a study of your community so that you can give a good overview of it to the persons the Pastor Search Committee is relating to. The community which your church serves is where you want to focus. In a large city, this will be limiting; but in a rural area you will want to be careful to encompass the total church field. For instance, open country churches often have members from nearby towns.

1. *General Characteristics*

In this section, you will want to classify your community in terms of downtown, neighborhood, suburban, small town, rural, etc. With this in mind, how old is the community? Is it transitional, or do you anticipate transition within a few years? What are the population figures for 1970, 1975, 1980, this year? What is the median age of the adult population? What dominates your community—one large industry, small industries, agriculture, or is it a "bedroom" for a neighboring city?

2. *The People of the Community*

First, give a general overview such as upper middle class, lower middle class, blue collar, or affluent. Then cover the employment characteristics such as pay scales, largely commuter or local, diversified among what types of industry. What about the mobility of the people? How large a percentage moves annually? What is the ethnic makeup of the community?

3. *Share something about the amenities of the community.*

Is decent housing available at a reasonable cost? How would you rate the public school system? Is there a college or university within fifty miles? What is the availability of medical care including hospitals, doctors and dentists? Is there the opportunity to "shop at home," or do you have to go elsewhere? What about the cost of living compared to other communities? Is this a place you like to call home?

4. *The Churches of the Community*

How many churches are there of your denomination? How many evangelicals are there of all persuasions? What is the dominant denomination of the area?

Keep in mind this may be more data than you will want to send to anyone except prospects. Also remember that this is going to be as valuable to you in gaining an understanding of your needs as it is to those who are helping you.

The Thrust Is Trust

Will the people you are going to be working with be able to trust your committee? Will they receive a true picture of your church not only from a historical perspective and the glorious promises of the future, but also the stark realities of the present?

Are you going to believe the people you depend upon for information? Will you accept the reliability of their opinions?

Keep in mind that this mutual trust is not only possible, but will come easily if you develop the methodology of chapter 2 and refine your efforts as suggested in this chapter.

Related Helps

Planbook

See chapter 3 for suggested committee activities and specific tasks.

Resource Kit

The Cassette gives further suggestions on how to give a candidate a clear picture of your church's place in your community.

4

Exploring with a Purpose

As soon as they settled deeply into their seats in the car, Mr. Mungo sighed and said, "I'm sorry I got us into that embarrassing situation. I just can't believe Brother Thomas would recommend the same man to two churches looking for pastors at the same time."

The committee had felt so confident as they had gradually joined together after the service at Central Church and by nods of the head and a few quiet exchanges had agreed to stop and talk to Pastor Louis about getting together for deeper conversations. They had been embarrassed to learn that the other small group hanging back was a Pastor Search Committee from a church in another city who were also planning to visit with Pastor Louis.

"Well, I'll have to admit this was a wild goose chase," muttered Mr. Johns, as the committee pointed their cars toward the airport to fly home. "I still can't believe Dr. Merle was not in his pulpit today. My friend who lives here in town checked on it and assured me he would be."

The other members of the committee did not say much, but they were already thinking about how to avoid such a waste of time in the future.

In still another church, Mrs. Egan summed up the feeling of the whole committee as they were meeting on Monday night. "We'll have to wait several weeks to get back in touch with Brother Fouts since their revival is in progress. I only hope we didn't hinder their revival by being in the service yesterday. I didn't think we would be so obvious but everyone noticed us."

The most basic step in exploring with a purpose is to be sure you have a person nailed down to explore with. In the three case studies, three separate problems arose; but there was a common cause for all three. There was no advance contact made with the candidate so that an interview could be arranged. This has been covered briefly in Steps 4 and 5 of Chapter 2 but needs more in-depth coverage at this point.

Scheduling the Interview

No prospect should be heard from the pulpit who is not also slated for an interview. If he is worth hearing, he is worth talking to. Since not all committees operate this way, you will want to stress this point when you contact him for permission to come. (See Step 5 of chapter 2.)

Normally it is best to line up the interview to take place immediately after the service you will attend. Since this is usually a morning service, the interview can often be combined with lunch. This is particularly helpful if the committee has traveled some distance. Factors which might affect this include the age of the children of the candidate and availability of a restaurant with privacy. An alternative will be to go to the prospect's home after all have completed lunch elsewhere. As much as possible, these matters should be settled in advance of the visit.

Releasing Tensions

To expect that there will be no tension in such a situation is to be completely unrealistic. You are dealing with the possibility of a person's making a major change in his personal life, his family life, and his pursuit of ministering under the will of God. On the other hand, your committee is facing up to the matter of what your church has asked you to do—search out God's choice for your church—and here is a real possibility.

You should assume primary responsibility for releasing the tension. You have called the meeting and have the most to gain from it. The most important thing is not to rush into heavy discussion. After the process of ordering and getting food served, you will have adequate time to ease into the interview. Be sensitive and, if more time is needed, take it.

Take the initiative in determining the content of the opening conversations. Learn more about the background of the candidate and his family. If you have accumulated a lot of information, check its accuracy by using it in discussion.

This is also an excellent time to have each person on the committee share something personal. This should include vocation, involvement in the church, length of membership, family, and so on. This will offer some points of reference to the prospective pastor when the more formal aspect of the interview takes place.

Making Use of Information Already Gathered

If the only exchange of information to this point has been the recommendation you have received and data from references, you are still in a position to set the direction of the interview. Your next step will be to share basic information about your church so the candidate can relate to the discussions that will follow.

In the Planbook there are suggestions for gathering and preparing materials about your church and community. When this is done as an integral part of the methodology of your committee, you have all of the necessary information needed to fully inform the person selected for an interview. Between the initial contact and the actual conclave, this material can be sent for study; thus time will be saved during the interview. You will also have shared more accurate information than can ordinarily be done orally.

Either way, the stage is set for you to gradually move into discussion of greater depth. It is at this time that you want to begin to ask questions about views of personal ministry and church organization and functioning. This is a person you have contemplated as a possible pastor, and it is imperative that you understand his views on these matters. Examples of questions are given in the Planbook.

Encouraging Openness

The committee sets the pace on this. You have already had the advantage of learning much about this person. Hopefully, you have shared some written information about your church. Now is the time for elaboration upon the matters that may have been unclear or misunderstood.

This is not to be done from the posture of attack or with the attitude of trapping the person in a deception, but simply from the position that you need more light on certain subjects.

The most effective way to do this is to encourage the person to talk. You will want to keep control of the direction of the conversations and be friendly but still give the candidate the opportunity to open up. He will be helped if the questions you intersperse call for narrative statements rather than simple opinions. For example, "Tell us how you work with church committees," not "Do you think committees are worthwhile?"

You have to be equally open during these hearings. When the interviewee asks a question about an embarrassing situation in your church, past, or present, you must give an honest answer. It may be that it is not appropriate to hang all the dirty linens out at this time, but you must acknowledge the reality of the problem and agree to further disclosure if this prospect becomes your selectee.

There is one other matter which may be appropriate at this time: the discussion of doctrinal matters. There are two schools of thought. The first is that doctrinal beliefs are of the utmost importance and must be cleared up before everything else. A possible answer to this is that earlier investigations would probably have revealed any unusual doctrinal views of the candidate.

The other school thinks that doctrinal matters can best be discussed after rapport has been developed between the candidate and the committee. Therefore, it is better to wait until a later interview, if indeed there is one, to get into doctrinal discussions.

People in both schools of thought agree that, when doctrinal issues are raised, they should be representative of the majority of the congregation and not a hobbyhorse of one or two people. However, if there is a vocal minority, this fact should be shared with an honest evaluation of the scope of the influence of the minority.

Recapping Assures Understanding

The first function in recapping is to resolve the simple issues that have been raised in the interview. Complex matters may need to be stated, but their resolution should not be attempted in haste. Simple issues usually come from listening to discussion and not being sure of the gist of what was said. A few follow-up questions will normally suffice.

The next course of action is to spend several minutes recapping what has been discussed. This is done in general terms but with specific points highlighted. The points of agreement may be jotted down for future use, and items which need possible further discussion should be noted.

According to the testimony of hundreds of ministers, one of the most miserable experiences they ever have is that of being left in limbo as to what to expect from Pastor Search Committees after being contacted. Though this is a natural consequence of the way some committees function, this should never happen.

Tell the prospect when he can expect to hear from you. Ordinarily, this will be after your next scheduled meeting. You will want to point out that if it is a negative response, it will be a note in the mail simply informing him that this is your decision.

If you are going to keep the person under consideration, this should be done by telephone. This will give the person an opportunity to express his continuing interest and let you tell him what the next step of the committee will be.

Related Helps

Planbook

Chapter 4 will help you over some rough spots in relation to this chapter in the Primer.

Resource Kit

Listen to the Cassette material on interviews for some brief case studies of classic problems between candidates and Pastor Search Committees before, during, and after interviews.

5

Pursuing Your Candidate

How to Decide Whether to Pursue

The most appropriate time to start the decision making process is immediately after the interview. If the committee is traveling together, it can be done as the group returns home. When this is not feasible, a meeting should be set as soon as possible in the week.

Sometimes the decision is very simple. There is quick and obvious consensus that the group does not wish to go any further with the person just interviewed. When this occurs, it will prove helpful for future deliberations to have some discussion on why this feeling exists. It is not necessary to be able to justify all of your reasons. Sometimes all you are able to determine is the simple absence of the continued leadership of the Lord in the relationship.

"I really feel good about that interview even though we have just agreed he is not the person for our church," mused John Downey. "Do you know why? Several years ago, I served on what was truly a pulpit committee. We went Sunday after Sunday to hear persons preach. We got to feeling guilty because no one pleased us. Without realizing it, we began to look for someone who simply was not bad. Finally, we hit upon this guy who did an adequate job, maybe even a little above average.

"We went back home and called him and told him we were

interested. He said he was also interested and agreed to come before the church. The church trusted us (and frankly were probably tired of us being out so often), so they called him. In three months, everyone knew it was wrong. But since we were all honorable people, we co-existed for three years.

"I feel good that the process we are following gives us reason to tell a man no, and I feel assured that we will know when to extend an invitation."

In other cases, a committee may not be able to come to any definite conclusion in their initial contemplations. If this lack of direction persists when the group has its formal deliberations at its regular weekly meeting, it is likely an indication that the person should be removed from further consideration. In the event of strong feelings by at least two of the committee, you may want to consider the first measure suggested in the section of this chapter on follow-up.

Besides some of the specific matters raised during the interview and regardless of whether this is done en route home or at a scheduled meeting, there are some other levels of discussion you need to have about the prospect and to a lesser extent his family.

With the limitations of a single interview and the acknowledgment that the discussion is highly subjective, there is nevertheless merit in evaluating personal characteristics as well as views of ministry. A problem in some of these areas can be a complete block to otherwise ideal approaches to ministry for your church.

You may think of others, but there are at least ten questions you will want to raise about each candidate.

1. How is his physical health? This may be a tender spot with some members of the committee because of personal problems, but that is not the question. The crux of the question is whether the prospect is physically healthy enough to perform the tasks of ministry which the congregation expects of him. There are several aspects to this. A person who doesn't care about his health (and many times the resulting physical appearance) may very well not care about other matters which are important to his ministry.

This does not mean, however, that you are to look for a health nut; they can cause problems equally limiting.

Anyone can experience illness. You are not looking for the person who has "never been sick a day in his life." For most this is unrealistic. Nor are you seeking to avoid people with handicaps. To the contrary, a person who has overcome a handicap and learned to compensate for it is often in superior condition otherwise.

Neither are you to be concerned with physical beauty or impressiveness. The world is full of successful leaders who are at both ends of the spectrum.

What you are doing is saying, "Taking the physical condition of this prospect and considering his attitude about it, can he do the pastoral ministries of our church?"

Fred Adams was anxious to change pastorates. He was moderately successful where he was, but his bouts with gastritus were increasing. He was sure a change of scenery would cure his ills.

The question is not just whether this would happen as the result of a move. It also must be whether he can make some changes in the way he cares for himself. If not, the problem will emerge sooner or later in a new field of ministry.

A person's physical needs must be met before he is capable of giving himself fully to his task.

2. How does he accept himself including his present limitations? Is he still growing in areas where growth is possible? One of the saddest situations in which a church can find itself occurs when the answer to these questions is negative.

Everybody has limitations, but the key is to be able to recognize them. Lack of recognition causes blind spots in ministry which always emerge as problems. On the other hand, knowing your limitations often gives you the opportunity to grow.

A case in point is a minister who feels completely inadequate in counseling young couples of this generation who have asked him to perform their wedding. He has three possible solutions. First, he can ignore his problem and their need. Second, he can arrange for someone else to do the counseling. Third, he can take advantage of a continuing education opportunity and study the latest in marriage counseling. Of course, the last is preferable. The counselees benefit, and he will probably grow more than just as a marriage counselor.

3. How resourceful is the candidate? This may be hard to determine in a first visit, but there should be at least one means of evaluation. Since your committee contacted him in advance about this visit, did he take advantage of the time? Did he independently seek out information about your church, or did he rely completely on the material you had furnished him? This characteristic will be important when he comes to the church field and begins to work. He should be self-reliant in seeking resources.

Edna Lange had been taken back by the question. Their candidate had raised the issue of the world mission support of the church for the past five years. It had declined. The committee knew it but had not spoken about it because they felt it would be solved if some other church problem were dealt with first.

How had he found this out, and why was he speaking confidently that he felt the matter should be of higher priority? As the pastor search committee had contemplated these matters, they realized they had been in contact with a person of many competencies.

Other candidates had the same resources available but had not used them or researched possible solutions. While they did not agree with all he had shared, they liked his willingness.

How consistent is the candidate in the way he administers his time and efforts in all aspects of life? Did you notice a particular sore spot? Did you get the feeling that if you disagreed on certain matters, it would be difficult to get along with him not only on this but perhaps many other things?

Did you notice an inordinate amount of interest by the candidate in a matter which could become avocational rather than a hobby? Were his job and family of proper importance to him?

"I wasn't as disturbed by his hobby as I was by the apparent cost of it and his attitude about it," said Del Trout. "He impressed me otherwise, but if we continue a relationship with Reverend Trotter I want to pursue this further.

"Since fishing is my hobby too I know something about the cost, and he has expensive equipment. Yet there are two other things that bother me even more than that." .

"I know what they are," chimed in Neal Stringer. "Even though he wanted to show us all his stuff, he was defensive about having it. I wonder why? Also, when someone asked his thirteen-year-old son about his fishing experiences his face was wreathed in disappointment." Neal turned to Del. "Am I right?" "Exactly. That's why we need to think about this and prepare to dig a little deeper."

5. How did you rate his interpersonal relationship skills? Besides with the Pastor Search Committee members (which might not be a true test), you should have had occasion to note how he related to his family and to church members. If you do not have a comfortable feeling about this, be sure you check it with other acquaintances.

The Bible admonishes us of the necessity for a pastor to get along well at home as well as with others. There are many churches today which give testimony to the fact that they did not give this sufficient attention. Later, much to their dismay, their witness in the community was hurt because of the pastor's problems of getting along.

The thing the committee talked most about as they drove home from their interview that Sunday afternoon was the contrast. Contrast was the word which kept slipping into their conversation as they thought about the Phillips family two weeks before and the Killian family that day.

No specific situation caused the uneasiness but rather the feeling that everyone in the Killian family was in fear of Reverend Killian. Two weeks before the physical tenderness had been very evident; today it had been obvious by its absence.

Before they changed subjects the committee wondered whether

they should even consider subjecting members of the congregation to such questionable behavior, even though they readily acknowledged the other skills of Reverend Killian.

6. How strongly does he stand behind his actions? There are always people ready to tell us what to do and perhaps even show us how to do certain things. However, they have problems when someone challenges the validity of the issue or the wisdom of the action.

While realizing that it is important that a person be able to admit a mistake, it is of the utmost importance that a minister stand behind his actions when he knows them to be right.

"Do you remember Quick Withdraw McGraw?" asked Don Boles of the other committee members. Two of them had been longtime members of Central Church as Don had, so they remembered. They told about Pastor McGraw, who had been at Central ten years previously.

They remembered that every time someone confronted his view on a matter, he dropped it. Often the matter being discussed was of importance to the church, but it went on Pastor McGraw's list of things "someone in the church had a hang-up about"; and he could never be drawn into discussion of it again.

"The man we interviewed today sure reminded me of Reverend McGraw," sighed Don Boles. The inference was clear.

It is impossible to effectively lead people and always be fearful of how they will respond on every issue, much less those of some controversy. Out of the background of information you receive about a candidate you should be able to have some discussions that will give you clues on this characteristic.

7. How flexible is he, and does he have a high tolerance for frustration? At first glance this seems contradictory to number 6. However, there are thousands of occasions in a pastor's ministry when flexibility is much more desirable than a stand.

Should the deacons' meetings be on Sunday afternoon or Monday night? This calls for flexibility, not rigidity. Should the youth of the church attend summer camp at Tonkawa or Pear Ridge?

This requires openness, not a closed mind. Even decisions such as who employs secretaries for the church should not become showdown issues.

Because these are matters for decision and because there are many more of greater and lesser importance, it is necessary that a minister not be easily frustrated. He has to have that ability to accept such matters as a part of his routine and not let them continually be sidetracking him from the weightier matters of ministry.

8. How effectively does he deal with his own mistakes? Though it is healthy to admit mistakes when they become apparent, it does not help to wallow in them. Mistakes are a daily part of life. This is especially true when one is living on the cutting edge as ministers are often called to do.

But mistakes can become debilitating if their reality becomes a source of guilt which never lets up. A minister, like all Christians, should be able to receive and accept forgiveness and move on to other opportunities.

"You sure put your foot in your mouth when you asked about who designed that pulpit stand," laughed John Longshore. "Yes, but we learned something from it," grinned Jake Shortner.

It seems the person responsible was their candidate. He had told them that the church called it Folsom's Folly. He had learned to live with it and could laugh about it.

This mistake had led them to talk about the subject, and Reverend Folsom shared with them about a problem he had made in regard to a staff position. The Pastor Search Committee was impressed with his ability to admit and work through his own mistakes.

9. How well does he grasp the reality of life? Some persons live in a dream world. They ignore the hard and unpleasant things of life. They simply refuse to acknowledge that these things exist.

Among ministers, this sometimes takes on the form of super-spirituality. To them, people don't have problems; they just aren't spiritual enough. There is enough truth in this to make it difficult to argue with. However, it does seem to ignore the reality principles found over and over in the Scriptures.

The church was obviously in bad shape. The congregation was but a handful; the building was in disrepair; and the neighborhood was uninviting.

As the committee began their interview with Reverend Holly, they had been impressed with his bubbly spirit and attitude. However, after a while, the committee members one by one had grown quieter. They were dismayed rather than amazed by the prospect. It was as though all the things so obvious to them did not exist.

This church was almost dead, and he would not even admit it was sick. The Pastor Search Committee knew their church needed help, and they also knew Holly could not help them.

10. How does he work in the present while planning for the future? It is easy to spot a person living in the past and to acknowledge his problems. It is important also that a person be examined as to how he relates the present with the future.

"I always wonder about a person who says, 'My ministry here is over,' " Mr. Wade said softly to the others in the group. "If it's over, why is the person still there?"

Mr. Wade is not a harsh, judgmental man by nature; so he was pressed for further comments.

He shared that he felt such an attitude was immobilizing. Nothing could be planned for the future, and there was no motivation to even maintain difficult programs.

He concluded by saying that he felt the Pastor Search Committee should avoid recommending a person who exhibited this type of leadership thinking.

A church is not going to move forward without a pastor who cares about what is happening now. However, he must care as well about what the church should be in the future. In fact, many times how effectively plans are made for the future become the turning points for the level of work today.

Not every person is going to be able to be evaluated by every one of these characteristics. However, there should be sufficient use of them to strengthen or weaken your basic feelings about the prospect's ministry capabilities.

"When Dr. Howard, our denominational consultant, told us that if we did our homework and used good methodology, the time would come when we would simply 'know' that we had found God's man for our church, I didn't believe him," exclaimed Thomas George. "I was a bit doubtful myself," agreed chairman Frank Michaels of University Church, "but I'm glad it's true." Mrs. Allison spoke up. "There have been times when I dreaded some of these meetings because it's been hard work, but I'm excited about tonight; what do we do next in our quest for Rev. Nathan Stephens?"

This is the experience every Pastor Search Committee looks for in one way or another. There is certainly a spiritual aspect to it, for the Holy Spirit must be working with a committee and a prospect. However, it must be emphasized there is the correct functioning of the committee in doing its task.

The Follow-up to the First Interview

The University Church made use of this course of action by setting a second conference with Reverend Stephens. Some churches go from a positive evaluation of a first interview directly to the last step suggested in this chapter. At least they do not schedule a second interview. Some make use of the telephone to gain any additional information they desire.

University Church was close enough to have another appointment. Besides, as they confessed to one another, they had not been willing to acknowledge how they had been moved the first time and wanted the reassurance of a second visit. Actually, a second visit was not a new experience for them; but the previous one had resulted in the termination of the relationship with the prospect.

In this particular situation, they heard candidate Stephens preach a sermon which was very different from the first. They also had the opportunity to get a little better acquainted with his family and had restricted the scope of their questions to a specific area of concern.

Yet Mrs. Allison did not say "Let's invite him before the church" but "what do we do next?"

The Transition from an Interview to a Contemplated Call

Interviews are done on a prospective pastor's home soil or on neutral ground. When a committee wants to expand that relationship, it is time to shift to the good earth of the community where the church is located. This action should be bypassed only in extreme conditions and limitations, and with full knowledge of the danger involved.

Frankfort Church skipped this measure because Mr. Meredith objected to the cost of having Pastor Melvin travel the four hundred miles twice. His contention was that this proposed visit to Frankfort could be combined with the visit in view of a call. He could come a day early and everything still be accomplished.

There turned out to be only one fly in the ointment. Pastor Melvin sent back his regrets the next week. He did not accept the call given to him by the church. While there is no way to guarantee that this will never happen, it should not happen in 99 percent of the cases. It should not have occurred at Frankfort.

The purpose of this transition visit is to give the prospective pastor (and ordinarily his wife) a chance to focus on what the opportunity really is which you as a committee are seriously offering to them contingent upon congregational action.

You have had discussions with them, furnished them information, and wooed them with accounts of the opportunities. But until they see and feel and experience the other sensations that can come only wth presence, they cannot make an intelligent response to a possible invitation.

Doubts are natural when any weighty decision has to be made. Even though they are natural, they must be resolved before the

Pastor Search Committee can be prepared to make a recommendation to the church.

Doubts are normally related to specific issues at this stage of work. Those kinds of doubts that "you can't put your finger on" will have already halted a relationship.

This is why the Frankfort Church had a bad experience. They asked the prospective pastor, themselves, and consequently the church to resolve its doubts and make a decision about a pastoral relationship without going through due process.

When it was all over, the committee admitted it knew the candidate would not accept the call even though they had gone through the motions of recommending him, and they were thankful he did not. Pastor Melvin also acknowledged he had made up his mind before Sunday, but felt obligated to go through the process and not embarrass the Pastor Search Committee. The result was that everyone's credibility was needlessly damaged.

The University Church Pastor Search Committee, as happy as they were about "knowing" they had found God's choice for their church, realized that these feelings had to be firmed up by further contact with Reverend Stephens. They quietly arranged for him to come to their city for what was still an unofficial visit.

Part of the committee met the Stephenses that afternoon when they got to town and took them on a tour of the community. After regular office hours at the church, they were given the opportunity to look over some basic records and see the facilities. Then they went to one of the committee members' home for dinner with the whole committee.

By the time dinner was over, all were aware that feelings had been firmed up. Indeed, it was time to finalize plans for an official visit.

Chairman Michaels took charge and went through the following process:

1. He asked that Reverend Stephens give brief answers to a series of questions concerning his understanding of salary, bene-

fits, present and future needs of the church, and also his direction of ministry.

2. He asked if he were ready to give an unequivocal commitment to officially come before the church "in view of a call."

3. Receiving a positive response, he led in a discussion of an appropriate date.

4. He asked their prospective pastor to meet with the church staff the next morning. A committee member went to the telephone and made the arrangements.

5. He led in the completing of agreements on reimbursement for the candidate's expenses which the committee had not been able to directly care for, possible moving plans, and what types of communication would be used during the interim of this visit and the official visit.

Reflections and Evaluations of This Process

Very fine work by a committee can be damaged if this function is not taken seriously. In all probability what seemed to be very positive relationships between a committee and a prospect have gone up in smoke at the last minute because of the neglect of this course of action.

In addition, numerous pastors have become disillusioned with new pastorates because of insufficient attention to this measure. These pastors thought they understood future intentions and accepted the call only to discover that there had been grave problems in communications with the Pastor Search Committee.

Two of the more controversial steps the University Pastor Search Committee took were asking for a commitment and arranging a staff visit. Regarding the former, the committee was not using coercion since they waited until the proper time to ask for the commitment. If a "prime" prospect is not ready at this stage to give unequivocal assurance that he will make an official visit, then the committee should begin to look for someone who will, even though it means their work is going to be extended. An official visit that has strings attached is not likely to result in an accepted call anyway.

The latter matter of the staff was not as much of a problem for University Church as it might be for others. University Church is a medium-sized church with an appropriately sized staff. The staff had worked hard while the church was pastorless, and there had been good communication and cooperation between the Pastor Search Committee and staff. The staff had been informed early in the process about how they would be treated when the Pastor Search Committee got to this point. They knew what to expect and what would be expected of them, particularly in the matter of keeping confidences.

This step does as much for the person being considered as it does for the committee. Not using it is often the reason a person turns down an invitation to come for an official visit with the whole church. Numerous cases can be documented of how this became the turning point for a prospect who felt an interest but was wavering.

Related Helps

Planbook

See chapter 5 for positive suggestions for dealing with tough questions at this stage of your work.

Resource Kit

Listen to the Cassette for further insights into handling this transitional period in a manner that benefits your committee, church, and candidate; familiarize yourselves with the two Bulletin Inserts planned for the Sundays prior to the candidate's official visit.

6

Sharing Your Investigations

"You have really helped us understand how pastors think when dealing with a Pastor Search Committee," commented Mrs. Spradlin, in evaluating a meeting with a consultant. The truth of this can easily be carried over into all the relationships in which a Pastor Search Committee finds itself. It helps everyone involved when there is understanding of how everyone is thinking, why they are responding as they are, when the committee will act, and what kind of actions to expect.

If there is one area in which committees have universally failed to give adequate consideration, it is in this area. Not that all committees have not communicated; but most committees do not formulate a plan as to how this will be done effectively. In reality, communication starts as soon as the committee is elected. However, the congregation is certainly willing to give the committee time to get organized and devise a plan of action.

Once this is accomplished, everyone involved is happier if communication guidelines are established and followed. The first thing agreed upon is the purpose of the committee. Many people, even after helping to elect a committee, do not fully understand the spiritual significance of their action.

As soon as this is done, then the congregation needs to know what its appropriate actions are in supporting the committee. Such matters as how to make recommendations, how to have input concerning pastoral qualities, and how to give appropriate prayer support will be immensely helpful to a caring congregation. This phase of communication exists throughout the life of the committee.

Another aspect of good communication involves assurance. A congregation needs positive reinforcement that everybody will be treated equally by the committee. This is to be true under all circumstances. A systematic giving of reports enables all members to know when they can receive information. Adequate notice concerning recommendations from the committee guarantees equal opportunity to respond to such actions.

Working hard on this objective guards the committee against antagonism by people who feel that they have been left out of rightful decision making and ensures the best possible response from the congregation at the critical points of your work.

In no way is this a suggestion that the congregation as a whole or any individual member has the right to know every act or decision of the committee. To the contrary, there is much which even family members of those serving on the Pastor Search Committee should not know. In fact, it is a gross injustice to allow someone to have information which they are not constrained by reason of their (lack of) position to keep private. For instance, a brother of a committee member cannot possibly feel the burden of the responsibility of serving on the committee. If he gets privileged news about the committee's actions, it is easy for him to inadvertently tell someone what he has learned. So it is best that wives, husbands, in-laws, and children not be told the inner workings of a committee.

Though it is necessary to keep much information confidential, you should not use this as an excuse for withholding all news of the committee's action from the congregation. Indeed, it should be the policy of the committee to give some sort of a report every week. There can be a lot of variety in how this is done.

First Steps

In chapter 1 we discussed how the committee develops an understanding of itself and how it relates to the congregation. In doing this, two very important steps in communication were taken. First, the Commissioning Service (see the Planbook) made the congregation extremely aware that you wanted them to be concerned and supportive of your efforts. You wanted spiritual rapport with them.

Second, in the use of the questionnaire, you let it be known that it was significant what the individual members considered to be of priority in how a pastor uses his time. When this is checked against your own perceptions, this gives a very fine vehicle for reporting to the congregation something of the direction the committee feels about the type of pastor to be sought. This indicates your openness to practical help (at least when asked for).

You allow the congregation to express itself concerning such matters as: (1) what the emphasis (or balance) should be in the preaching ministry. (2) what are needed ways of strengthening the fellowship of the church. (3) what gaps in pastoral leadership need to be closed. (4) what can be done to have maximum coverage in ministering to the total congregation. (5) what organizations of the church need strong pastoral support.

Another benefit from this step is that it helps the congregation to know that the committee is not hemmed in by the usual stereotyped profile of a pastor. One committee who had simply asked the people to tell them what kind of pastor they desired came up with an almost completely negative profile. He was to be "not too young," "not going to school," "should not preach long sermons," "not have a large family" (obviously this was not a small town where school enrollment was watched), and "had to be a good mixer." Thus your reply to someone's query "What kind of pastor are we looking for?" is that the profile gained from the questionnaire will be used as your guide.

Don't Miss This Opportunity

Misunderstanding can easily develop between the general membership and the committee when recommendations are being received for prospective pastors. To avoid misunderstanding, clear-cut guidelines must be given to the people as to how recommendations will be received. Though this is the imperative action needed, it is helpful if it is shared with the people how recommendations will be processed once received. (See chapter 2.)

An effective way of communicating this is by making use of an available bulletin board within the church. On this board (the most prominent available), display can be arranged of all the forms which the committee will be using in the recommendation procedure. (See chaps. 2 and 3.)

Caution should be taken to do a good job. One committee became so sold on this idea that they rushed out and tacked up several forms on the main bulletin board of the church. Unfortunately, there was already a very nice mission offering promotion which was designed to use the whole board. Not only did the forms look out of place, but the person who had spent considerable time on the mission project was somewhat offended.

If there is no one on the committee with the skills to create an attractive bulletin board, someone from outside the committee should be enlisted. They should be given a theme such as "Your Pastor Search Committee" or "Your Pastor Search Committee at Work." You will want to display all of the necessary materials for that stage of the process.

The most appropriate approach is to show the chronological process which the committee is following. This will aid the person who had made a recommendation in understanding why committee action cannot be completed in a week or ten days. The bulletin board might be designed in this manner.

Bulletin boards have not been popular communication vehicles for Pastor Search Committees; but, done well, they can be an effective device. Two cautions should be taken. Never leave the same information up for more than three weeks. (It may be repeated later.) Also, be sure the work is neat even if it cannot be artistic.

Sorting Through the Recommendations

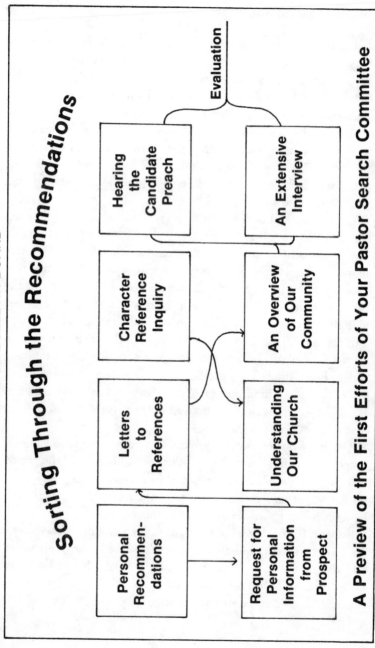

Personal Recommen- dations	**Letters to References**	**Character Reference Inquiry**	**Hearing the Candidate Preach**
Request for Personal Information from Prospect	**Understanding Our Church**	**An Overview of Our Community**	**An Extensive Interview**

Evaluation

A Preview of the First Efforts of Your Pastor Search Committee

Avoid This Communication Barrier

Once a committee gets past the information gathering stage, the temptation to "clam up" is almost overwhelming. As strong as this urge is, it must not be allowed to happen. Everything that has been accomplished with the earlier steps to establish rapport and trust with the congregation will be lost. When clamming up occurs, two things can happen. First, if the process begins to take more time than the congregation has been accustomed to in the past, pressure will be applied to the committee to act faster. Second, when you do get ready to present a candidate to the church, you will have to attempt to communicate with a group who is not as prepared as they should be or could be for such an event.

Positively, when a committee keeps the lines open with the congregation during the period between "nominations and election," the base of congregational support can be constantly enlarging. The surprising thing about this is that less factual information is actually being dispersed than at any other time. You are basically saying, "We are still at work and we are dependent upon your prayer support." Of course it cannot be said this same way every time, and small bits of information should be added at appropriate times such as "We will visit our first prospect in two weeks" or "We have decided to have more extended interviews with someone within this month."

No information meant for committee ears and eyes alone is given out; yet the people are constantly (weekly) being told, "we know we are serving you and we want your support."

Repetition will be needed at this point if this feeling of openness is to reach all members of the congregation. Thus, announcements should be made during regular church services and in printed media such as bulletins and newsletters. This should be done on a weekly basis with all committee members taking part. What will be said is always a group decision. Making this decision can be a good way to conclude weekly committee meetings because it will have the added benefit of making the committee take stock of its progress to that point.

Make the Most of This Event

The committee can truly draw the congregation to a new high in interest and anticipation when it is ready to present the person selected as the prospective pastor. This interest and anticipation can in turn be used as a unifying force which will be beneficial to the church and pastor together in future days.

A word of caution is in order. This time of presentation will be effective only if there is complete agreement by the candidate and the committee on all matters without coercion on the part of anyone. Numerous churches and pastors have been embarrassed by a last-minute withdrawal caused by misunderstanding or excessive pressure.

However, when that moment comes that a committee knows beyond doubt that it has found God's choice for their church, you have reached an exciting plateau in your job. Presuming communication has been maintained with the people in (and out of) the pew, it will be easy to get matching anticipation from the church body.

It cannot be stressed too strongly how important it is to respond to this openness. The congregation has maintained a spirit of trust and has withheld its natural inquisitiveness; now the committee must give them *all* available information.

"All available information" means that the congregation is virtually inundated with all the data the committee has gained about the person and his family. A rule of thumb is "if it was important for the committee to know, it probably should be shared with the congregation." Certainly you should have nothing to hide. If you do, that is a sure sign of trouble for the future. You will need to develop personalized information and print it in newsletters, bulletins, and special mailings. This same news will be shared orally in every meeting of the congregation.

However, besides this, two special bulletin inserts are available which are designed to aid in general preparation for hosting a prospective pastor.

In the two- to three-week period of telling the people the good news about the prospective pastor, there should be a steady progress toward the weekend the candidate will be present. It is the responsibility of the committee to give the congregation a chance to get to meet the prospective pastor as well as to hear him.

An informal gathering of the church membership on Saturday is one of the most effective communication devices you will use. People are much more open to a person whose hand they have shaken and with whom they have chatted for even a few seconds. Then they are not seeing a stranger walk into the pulpit on Sunday morning but someone they know. It is really not important how long they have known him. Naturally, this also has the same type of effect upon the person entering the pulpit.

It may be that the person coming in view of a call will want to talk with a specific group within the church, such as the deacon body or all Sunday School workers. If this is so, this time should be on Sunday afternoon. This is as soon as any group will be knowledgeable enough about the prospect to discuss matters of any importance.

Decision Time Demands Your Best

When the time comes that a church is ready to vote, it is entering into a vital communication procedure. The Pastor Search Committee will be telling the congregation, "We have done what you have asked us to do. We have searched out God's choice for our church, and we present him to you without reservation." The congregation will be expressing its will in a tangible manner. By doing so it will be giving approval (or disapproval) to the efforts of the Pastor Search Committee. It will be stating its belief in the person who has opened his life to them to serve as pastor.

The person will respond to the action of the church with a commitment to take up his service to God with these people.

Because this is such a vital step in the very life and history of the church, every measure should be taken to ensure utmost participation by the membership. This begins with the basics. *When* will the vote be taken? *How* will the vote be taken? *Who* will want to cast votes? *What* will be the procedure for announcing the vote? These questions must be answered in oral announcements and in the various printed pieces the church normally uses, such as newsletters and bulletins. The committee should climax its efforts on the matter with a letter to all the membership and by a final public announcement on Sunday morning.

No Time for a Lapse

Committees have been known to do their job very effectively through the issuing to the call of the church and then slip off into relative obscurity. To do so is to abdicate a communication responsibility. You need to help the congregation begin to accept the person called as pastor. A vote to call does not necessarily mean everyone is fully prepared to accept the person. The time between the call and the move to the church field should be used wisely. Some people will want to know what they can do in a concrete manner; provide food, help unload furniture, babysit, and so on. Others need to know what they can do to be prepared spiritually, mentally, and emotionally for the experience of having a "new" pastor.

People should not be expected to know these things automatically. For some, it will be a first-time experience. With others, it may be that though they have been around when a new pastor came, this is the first time they have been aware that it is a special experience. Then there are always those who have only seen it done wrong, even when intentions were right.

The bulletin inserts written for this time in the life of a church will be beneficial. They are a part of your resource kit.

All of this should be climaxed with a very special Sunday when the pastor assumes the position to which he has been called. In the actions of the day (described elsewhere in this book), the committee assists the pastor and people to begin with openness to each other that will be far-reaching in its consequences.

The countryside is littered with committees who attempted to bypass some of these communication processes. Their whole efforts exploded in their faces because of indifference at some vital point which did not seem to them to be that necessary at that moment. Sometimes the casualties included ministers who were involved, and at other times a whole congregation has been emotionally ambushed.

The acceptance of the responsibility to serve on the Pastor Search Committee included (whether you knew at the time or not) accepting the old adage of "praise the Lord and tell the people." Actually you must go further; you must see that the people understand what you are telling them as you progress through each step of the pilgrimage of being a Pastor Search Committee member.

Related Helps

Planbook

Chapter 2 specifically relates to this chapter.

Resource Kit

Make use of the Posters, the Bulletin Inserts, the Cassette, and the Special Service Outlines at this stage of your work.

7

Presenting the Person

The Pastor Selection Committee
is pleased to announce that
Dr. Conlan Baldwin
will assume the pastorate
of Grace Church
Sunday, August 3, 1979

This announcement in a church newspaper was the first the members of Grace Church had known about the new pastor. The practice of simply announcing a new pastor is beginning to take place, evidently with the blessings of the congregations involved.

A Contrasting Method

The illustration above is a rather extreme way of presenting a new pastor to a church. While this extreme may not be a temptation to a Pastor Search Committee in contrast to a Pastor Selection Committee or the old Pulpit Committee, there are some related problems which may slip into your thinking.

The thinking in its less insidious form says, "The congregation has given us a job to do. They have trusted us. We have found the person; now let's get on with getting him called as pastor and then get his work under way." This should sound familiar to thousands who have served on Pastor Search Committees, but let's look deeper at what is being said. The most important part of the statement is "the congregation trusts us." That trust is not directed simply toward your ability to find a person who is willing to serve as pastor, but also that church members trust you to do it in such a way as to gain their confidence and give them the right to express that confidence by means of a ballot. They also trust you to help them to be sufficiently informed to make that decision.

By the time your committee is ready to make a recommendation, you have become personally acquainted with the person you contemplate presenting. You have been with him (and his family) in worship, in face-to-face interviews, around a fellowship meal, and probably in other situations. You are comfortable with the relationship. But there is a great gulf between you and the general membership since they have not had these advantages.

This cannot be passed over lightly. There is a very strong relationship between how a person is made known to the congregation and how quickly and effectively he will be able to relate to them as pastor. Besides the communication techniques in the previous chapter, this is the Pastor Search Committee's first opportunity to introduce the individual they believe to be God's choice for their church to the whole church.

Using the Time Wisely

Two types of exposure are needed to effectively acquaint the prospective pastor with the general congregation. They should be done in logical sequence and require two days in order to be done considerately and thoughtfully. Therefore, plans should be made to have the prospective pastor and his family in town by midday Saturday.

Arrival by this time will allow for sufficient rest before the activities begin that evening. They can check into the motel and have an update session with the committee chairman, but should not be further involved for the afternoon unless they request it.

The first exposure is by means of an icebreaker type of event. It should be at the church (in the fellowship hall, if possible) and completely informal. The time of year will influence what type of

food is included, but it should be something the church membership generally responds to. A reception is not ordinarily successful
because it has built-in limitations about how people get acquainted.

An extremely large church or a church with a large number of
older members will want to consider two get-acquainted sessions.
One could be in the afternoon to accommodate those who find it
difficult to get out at night. There should be a break lasting several
hours between the two.

One of the purposes of this cultivative open meeting is to reduce
tension. It is impossible to have this situation of a person and a
congregation both being in a life-changing decision time and
there not be tension. But the tension can be lessened if your committee works at it.

In the mind of the average church member the question is,
"How can I know whether to give my support to this person? I
don't call someone 'Pastor' easily." On the other hand, the candidate is saying to himself, "How do I know if I will be able to minister to these people? The committee is great, but are the rest of
the church members like them?"

Seeing one another across a pulpit will not answer these questions completely. This is why many individuals in the congregation (where this is their only exposure to the prospect) are often
supercritical. It is also the reason many pastors still "put out the
fleece" or set certain conditions of response in advance which
must be met. It is a way to cope with uncertainty.

However, when the same people peer at one another across the
same pulpit, but have met (however briefly), shaken hands, and
called each other's name, it is different. They are not strangers siz-
ing one another up. They have had what the Pastor Search Committee has told them about each other positively reinforced. The
pastoral bond is not there yet, but each is beginning to see how it
can be a reality.

The second exposure is in a worship service or, better, in two
services. With some barriers down, the guest should be able to

preach with more freedom and the congregation able to listen with more openness.

In a book which has seemingly taken some of the spotlight off the pulpit in the proposed methodology, it perhaps seems strange to find advocation for the prospective pastor preaching in a second worship service. This, of course, would be advisable only in churches where such opportunity presents itself in one day. Many of the churches using this material have evening worship services; and when this is true, there is a distinct advantage to having a second sermon.

The advantage is that night services are usually less formal. Thus the sermon can be preached in a different atmosphere and can possibly be another type of sermon. This broadens the knowledge from which the congregation will make its decision.

Providing Fairness at Decision Time

This is primarily a chronological process. The Pastor Search Committee sets the date with the person you aspire to recommend and then works the planned sequence of events back from that weekend. Naturally, the selected date has to be distant enough to allow for the proposed interim events.

Now is not the time to become impatient. You are still at a critical time in seeking to close the gap of knowledge between you and the congregation.

The set date is the date when the congregation votes on the recommendation of the Pastor Search Committee. It may be the same date as other events; but if not, it takes precedence in planning.

Here is how Grace Church handled this aspect of enlightening the church about the person they were recommending as pastor.

At the close of their transitional, on-the-site interview with Pastor Kereth, the question was raised about the most appropriate time for Pastor Kereth to officially appear before the church. Mrs. Galen raised the issue about when the church would vote, feeling this would have influence upon when the visit should be. Her question seemed providential since there were several matters about voting which had not been resolved. Fortunately, the by-laws of the constitution of Grace Church were not restrictive and gave the Pastor Search Committee the right to make a recommendation about voting procedures, provided a three weeks' notice was given. Vice-Chairman Evans had been investigating possible voting procedures and shared these with the committee.

1. *Procedure 1:* The vote is taken after a lapse of time following the official visit. This is most often one week. Mr. Evans told the group he had recently read an article which pointed out that in the average congregation on a given Sunday, at least 30 percent of those present had not been present the previous Sunday. This plan raised the possibility of a significant number of people voting who were at best less informed, if not uninformed.

Procedure 2: Though there was not a delay in voting, under this plan there was a predetermined percentage of votes which had to be favorable. Investigation revealed this ranged from 75 to 90 percent. Mr. Evans observed that this seemed to be contrary to the openness which the committee had sought, but he had never-theless checked further. A denominational representative had pointed out that this allowed for minority rule, which was contrary to congregational polity. Indeed, a church in a neighboring town had let an 11 percent negative vote negate the work of many months. He had checked with their interim pastor and found that many pastors would not allow themselves to be considered by a church with such a policy.

Procedure 3: The vote is taken at the conclusion of the last service in which the prospect participates. There are no advanced restrictions, and the votes are tallied and announced immediately. Mr. Evans acknowledged some early misgivings about this procedure, but shared that as he had prayed about it, he had concluded that it was an extension of their policy of openness. He said to the congregation very effectively, "We have sought to do our job, and we trust you to make the right decision."

After discussion the committee and Pastor Kereth agreed that

Proposition 3 had the most merit and would be their procedure.

"In what form will the committee recommendation be made to the congregation?" was Mrs. Flake's question. "I know there is no set formula for this, but I do have one basic idea. The recommendation should be written."

There is much merit in Mrs. Flake's thinking. This is not a time for misunderstanding. You may say, "We're from a small church, and all we need to say is that we recommend Brother Smith at the same salary which our last pastor received."

That is a simple statement, but let's look a bit deeper into it. First, a poll of the whole congregation would probably reveal that at least 50 percent do not know what salary was paid the last pastor. Then suppose you included the salary figure. That could still be inadequate. What does that figure represent? Total benefits? Base salary only? How does the parsonage (or lack of one) fit into the picture?

A larger church will have these questions and even more to answer for the congregation. The most effective way to do this is in written form.

The Pastor Search Committee of Grace Church wishes to make the following recommendations:

1. That we call Rev. Robert Edwin Kereth to serve as pastor of Grace Church.

2. That he be called at an annual compensation of $00,000. The compensation includes the following:

Salary	00,000
Housing Allowance	0,000
Self-Employment Tax	0,000
Hospitalization (family)	0,000
Annuity and Retirement, disability	0,000

3. That the cost of automobile operation for carrying out church ministries be 00 costs per mile for the balance of this year with a monthly stipend to be set in the next church budget.

4. That the following time compensations be included:

One weekday be taken when not preempted by any of the following:

Five Sundays per year
> Two of which *must* be included in three weeks of
> vacation.
> One of which *must* be spent visiting another
> church for observation purposes.
> Two of which are discretionary for revivals or
> either of the purposes above.

Twenty days per year for continuing education opportunities. (These shall normally be weekday events.)
Other time as granted by the church through normal
procedures of adapting church policy.

5. That the church pay the cost of having a professional mover
relocate Reverend Kereth and his family to our city, where he will
minister at Grace Church.

6. That if the church approves all other listed aspects of this
recommendation, Pastor Kereth begin his official duties five Sundays from today, which would be ___(date)___ .

This led the committee back into the process of establishing a
time schedule. If everybody in the congregation had equal opportunity to hear at the same time about the prospective pastor, the
committee would be doing all it could.

The agreement was made that Pastor Kereth would be with
them four weeks from the coming weekend. The sequence of
events would begin the following Sunday with a statement that
an announcement would be made the following Sunday morning
about the identity of the person to be recommended. It was
further announced when the vote would be taken; and this statement was made in every meeting of the congregation over the next
three weeks. The process was now in gear.

Related Helps

See chapter 6 for additional ideas for handling this occasion with dignity and making it meaningful for all concerned. Sample communications are included.

Resource Kit

Listen to the Cassette for further information on such matters as the role of an interim pastor on this occasion, dealing with constitutional hindrances, and handling last-minute crises; use the two Bulletin Inserts designed for the Sundays prior to the candidate's official visit.

8

Solidifying Your Efforts

Nothing is more satisfying in a task than the completion of it. Sometimes completion brings mixed emotions because it is hard to give up something that has become a very large part of your life. Still, there is true contentment in knowing you have taken on a responsibility and seen it through to the end.

Maintaining Your Quest for Excellence

Any Pastor Search Committee which has reached this stage of its work knows how many temptations have popped up along the way. The temptations have commonly been to cut some corners in some of the methods being used. The enticement to begin taking shortcuts when the end is in sight is almost overwhelming.

Sometimes you will experience guilt feelings about it, but these can be rationalized away fairly easily. After all, you have worked hard and long, and now it is time for some others to get involved. Your rationalizations are partly true—you do need to begin to involve others. However, you must stay vitally involved for a bit longer.

Your prospect has received and accepted the call of a church. This is no time for a Pastor Search Committee to ease up in its quest for excellence. You have stayed on track in the past when it would have been easy to jump off, and you will want to stay on track now.

Your goal is in sight—God's choice in a happy pastoral relationship in your church. You have done some hard work in the past months, but you have been willing to do it because you believe in your church and believe that God wants to use it.

There are still some steps to take to assure that your goal will be reached. No one else can do some of these things, and no one can do them as well as you. There is one further reason for pressing on in your quest for excellence.

Over the past months you have developed a relationship with the other members of the committee. This is a very important experience in your life. The culminating group experience should be one of excellence in solidifying your efforts.

Checking Your Punchlist

One of the early analogies used about the work of the Pastor Search Committee related to the construction of a building. If that can be picked up again, you are at the stage of checking for items that were in the plans but may have been overlooked or not done correctly. In the building industry, the list which evolves from such an inspection is commonly called a punchlist.

Builders know that though they may have done a very solid job otherwise, if they fail to deal wisely with this list, they can have long-term problems. The very fact that an item makes a list is indicative of its importance even though it may seem petty to some.

Here are some matters you may want to think about to see if you have need of developing a punchlist.

1. *Has the congregation given approval of all agreements that have been made with the new pastor?* You are basically right when you say that should have been done before the call. There are two reasons to look into this matter at this late date.

The first reason is that some phase of the agreements may have been overlooked when these matters were presented to the church earlier. The worst thing that can be done is to gloss over it, act as though it didn't happen, and hope it will never be discovered. Deal with the matter forthrightly. Go to the congregation and acknowledge the oversight or error, as the case may be. Then seek their approval. If approval is given, the matter can be closed. If it is not, then the new pastor should be notified immediately. Chances are very high that he will be understanding at this point, but delay will only bring problems.

The second reason for checking on agreements in these latter stages is that some agreements are negotiated after a call. This can happen even when a committee is very thorough in its efforts. Examples might be an increase in hospitalization insurance, a request for delaying the move for two weeks, or a decision by the Pastor Search Committee (based on their own late research) to recommend a plan for annual continuing education leave. No matter how insignificant these matters may seem to some, they deserve congregational action.

You might also want to keep in mind that these late-appearing agreements need to be brought to the church by committee action. Besides being poor polity, there is also the possibility of hurt feelings if one or two members of a Pastor Search Committee act on behalf of the whole.

A sure way to see a matter lose support is to hear a committee member oppose it in an official congregational meeting because he was uninformed.

2. *Have you provided for an orderly plan of moving the new pastor and his family?* This is going beyond the basic agreements and checking on your plan of action.

Trinity Church is a church of sound financial strength located in a medium-sized city. When they recently called a pastor, they provided for his family in a very fine way except for one thing. They decided to move him rather than employing a professional mover. Their decision proved to be almost disastrous when one of the trucks they had borrowed caught on fire. Fortunately, there were no major losses.

Calling a pastor means commitment of resources, and this commitment should start in the relocation process. Unnecessary cutting of expenses at this time is debilitating to a new pastor and his family. They have been treated royally in the courting process;

and now it seems that since they have accepted the call, all expressions of caring have been cut off.

Other costs in moving often include motel costs at either or both ends of the move, temporary housing, and meals en route or while waiting to complete the move.

One additional provision which should be made for the family is people. That is, identify people of your church who are willing to assist. This is one of those ways you can begin to broaden the involvement of the membership. It can also be a means of saving money, although this should not be the primary motive.

When the moving van arrives, there should be church members present whether it is a parsonage or a home bought by the pastor. They should be there not to do the moving of furniture or even assist in the moving, but to be of help to the family. It may be that caring for children would enable the wife and mother to get a lot more done. Running errands to such places as a hardware store can be a great time saver. Even providing pet care might be significant to some families. Food is always a need. Planning with the new family about how they would prefer help be provided can be an asset.

3. *Have you correlated the plans for the first Sunday with the new pastor and the congregation?* The first day of ministry is a very special day to a new pastor. He is the one in the spotlight, but it should be as special to the congregation as it is to the pastor. Some churches will need to be encouraged to look upon it as being that notable an occasion. You will want to assume that responsibility if it is needed.

One way to help give it significance is to ask the pastor not to assume any pastoral duties until that first Sunday. His preparation for that day is not likely to be impaired if this is done.

The congregation can be drawn into the particular value of the day if they are informed about what will be done and how desirable their participation really is. Besides making them feel wanted, be sure they understand the spiritual aspects of the event.

4. *Have you scheduled a meeting with the pastor in the early*

part of his first week? Any sense of threat or negativism can be laid aside if this is done in advance.

Putting on the Finishing Touches

Contentment in the membership should be the first gift of a church to a new pastor. This has been one of the aims of the methodology suggested throughout this book. The last two involvements of the Pastor Search Committee are your efforts to preserve the work you have done. The first of the two puts the shine on, and the second hardens (permanentizes) the gloss.

That Special Day

1. *The covenant service*—This is designed to deepen the commitments which have already been made leading up to and including the call of the church and the acceptance of the pastor.

By this time, there is some understanding of what the direction and focus of the church should be for the future. This service enjoins the pastor and people to work together for the realization of their goals and dreams.

There should be an element of time commitment also in service. It is difficult to pin down, but all should be aware that lofty and worthwhile goals are not hastily done.

2. *The time for dialogue*—This must be done under strong guidelines, but there should be an hour set aside for the general membership to raise questions of importance for the new pastor.

A good moderator is a must. Some will come only to express their prejudices or biases rather than to take part in a learning and sharing experience.

3. *The sermon(s) of the day*—As soon as possible after the call the pastor should be told about the plans for the first Sunday. (Some committees will find opportunity even earlier.)

The matter of suggestions for sermons particularly needs to be attended to quickly. It will be a challenge for some to switch from their favorite first sermon, but this is an integral part of the special Sunday. Suggestions should be made that the sermon(s) be along the line of "My Goals in Ministry at ____(church)____" or "The Future of the Local Church."

4. *The reception or get-acquainted function*—This particular reception is for the church family. Another one later on may be planned for the community as a whole or for invited guests from other churches and community organizations.

Small and medium-sized churches may prefer to have a get-acquainted party rather than a reception. This affords the opportunity for the new pastor to learn names and faces much more rapidly than is possible in a walk-through reception.

This can be done in several ways, but one of the most effective ways combines the old-fashioned pounding with getting acquainted. The pastor and his family are seated in the part of fellowship hall where they can see the crowd and can be seen and heard. The congregation sits in alphabetical groups according to family names, that is, A—C, D—G, H—L, and so on. Each family goes forward and tells the pastor, "We have a bag of apples because our name is Ames," "We have a box of soap because our name is Southerland," and so on. Each family member is introduced at the same time.

Large churches can do this over an extended period of time by using established groupings of adults as the basis for setting up the get-acquainted sessions. This plan tends to include people who would not be as comfortable in introducing themselves to the new pastor if they had to initiate the occasion. Also people appreciate having their name known, and this aids the new pastor in making that step toward acceptance.

The Time to Say We're Not Special

As the pastor closed the door behind him, he blurted out, "There is a person in our church giving me all kinds of trouble and you would never guess who it is." The denominational worker looked at the pastor and asked one question which drew him up sharp. "Is it the chairman of the Pastor Search Committee or just one of the members?" "It's one of the members, but how did you know? Has someone been in talking to you?"

The denominational employee/friend assured the pastor that he hadn't been approached, and then recounted to him that he had known numerous pastors who had experienced similar difficulties.

The pastor had one more question. "Up until two months ago, he was one of my best friends and our families spent time together almost every week; why the sudden change?" "Did you break off the weekly visits about four months ago?" asked his friend. A simple nod of the head affirmed his suspicions.

What was behind this episode and all the others like it? One thing basically, but with a predictable side-effect.

The Pastor Search Committee had not made a formal effort to transfer the special relationship they had built up with the new pastor to the congregation as a whole. This caused the following sequence of events.

1. The new pastor was called and accepted.

2. The Pastor Search Committee said, "Our work is done."

3. The new pastor moved on the field and began his ministry.

4. When he needed some advice on church matters, he turned to the Pastor Search Committee chairman because he knew him and felt comfortable with him as a confidant.

5. When the pastor and his wife were ready to spend some recreation time, they turned to a committee member and his wife who had given them a lot of attention since their arrival. This couple became their best friends.

6. As the months passed, the pastor found he had numerous people in the church he could seek advice from. The former Pastor Search Committee chairman accepted this as a natural occurrence.

7. The pastor and his wife began to feel that they should have a wider range of social contacts among the membership. The couple who had been so close felt that this was an unjust slight and lack of gratitude for all they had done. In four months, friendship turned to hostility.

Two things are obvious about what happened. First, better communications could have eased the situation considerably in most cases. Second, the reactions could have been reversed. That is, the chairman could have had his feelings hurt about losing his role as confidant, and the committee member could have understood about the change in social relationships. Actually, there did not have to be a problem; but there was one, and will be one quite often in similar situations. It is necessary to take steps to defuse such potentially explosive situations.

This is why it was on the suggested punchlist earlier in this chapter to have a meeting with the new pastor after his first Sunday. You let him know your basic intentions prior to this meeting.

The agenda for the meeting where you share your termination plans is very simple. You have a time of sharing with the pastor the blessings you have received as committee members of working together and of finding God's will which has culminated in his presence as pastor. You then, in a way which is meaningful to you, ask him to take the mantle you have worn as a committee and hold it over the whole congregation. Simply stated, you declare yourselves not to be special.

There is one school of thought which contends that the Pastor Search Committee should remain intact as a group. The idea is that the pastor needs someone to go to for evaluation of his ministry. If this is done, there could still be the session previously proposed but with the agreement to meet every six months to function as group evaluators.

However this last matter is handled, the final act of the Pastor Search Committee is to send a message to the congregation expressing appreciation for the privilege of serving and encouraging them to accept your new pastor as God's choice for our church.

Related Helps

Planbook

See chapter 6 for further ideas on completing your job in such a way as not to invite future problems.

Resource Kit

Listen to the Cassette for alternate ideas on the activities involved in completing your task; use the two Bulletin Inserts related to accepting and helping the new pastor.

Epilogue

"It sounds good, but is it worth the effort?" is probably what is going through your mind right now. You will be the final judge about that, but the only legitimate way you can make your judgment is to give a 100 percent effort.

In the period of time this material has been written, I have personally been involved in counseling with pastor-friends who have been in negotiations with committees from churches seeking pastors. I wish I could say that all the experiences had been happy.

The truth of the matter is that the feelings were the same in both types of situations. That is, the committees in all cases felt that they had found God's choice for their church. Some had not been able to communicate their feelings to the church body and so had experienced the rejection of their candidate.

A committee can accept almost anything else which happens to them better than the congregation refusing to accept their "final" recommendation.

Yet as the accounts of the matters which had taken place in the negotiation process were recounted to me, it was obvious that the Pastor Search Committee members were largely responsible for the negative results. At one key spot after another in the process of the methodology, they had taken shortcuts which came back to haunt them. They had set in motion negative feelings and ideas which would emerge later in the process.

God intervenes in the work of a Pastor Search Committee as he does in all areas of our life. We should be very thankful for this.

However, I fear we often use the Lord for an excuse for our own failures.

When a committee makes a good solid effort based upon proven principles and workable methodology, 99 percent of the time when they present the person they believe to be God's choice for their church, the congregation is going to agree with them.

Checklist for Committee Members

What's My Score?

____	____	*On the Matter of Enthusiasm and Dedication*
____	____	Do I show enthusiasm for my work?
____	____	Does the rest of the committee have enthusiasm?
____	____	Have we convinced ourselves that we want God's choice as our pastor and not just an acceptable person?

		Building a Good File of Prospects
____	____	Have we stayed with the principles agreed upon for recommendations?
____	____	Have we been faithful to check references?
____	____	Are we staying up to date?

		What Kind of Image Are We Giving to the Congregation?
____	____	That we are being faithful to our task?
____	____	That we want them to know every step of importance?
____	____	That we understand their desires for a pastor?

		Are We Being Resourceful with Gathering of Information Needed About:
____	____	Church records and statistics

____	____	Church history
____	____	Church organization structures
____	____	Community growth
____	____	Community resources
____	____	Community (and church) potential

How Did You Score Overall?
Check one:

___great ___satisfactory ___pretty good ___room for improvement
___must try harder

Great or Satisfactory deserve a pat on the back; anything less means that you have just begun. Would you agree that greater effort is needed?